The New
PLAYMAKING

The Latest in the Integration of the Arts in Education

by

CREATIVE
EDUCATIONAL
SYSTEMS

THE NEW
PLAYMAKING

The Latest in the Integration of the Arts in Education

by

Creative Educational Systems

THE NEW
PLAYMAKING

The Latest in the Integration of the Arts in Education

by

Creative Educational Systems

© Copyright 1991, 1993 by Creative Educational Systems
Printed in the United States of America

Published by:
Dovehaven Press
P.O. Box 6659
East Brunswick, NJ 08816

Library of Congress Cataloguing-in-Publication Data
The New Playmaking: The Latest in the Integration of the Arts in Education by Creative
Educational Systems

                p. cm.
       Includes bibliographical references and index.
       ISBN 0-942345-10-x (pbk) : $20.00
         1. Arts—Study and Teaching—United States. 2. Creativity in art.
I. Creative Educational Systems (Staten Island, New York)
1993
371.3'32—dc20
Library of Congress Catalog Card Number   93-71858

A BRIEF HISTORY OF CREATIVE EDUCATIONAL SYSTEMS

In 1978, David Rockefeller wrote: "Art is the nourishment of the soul." This widely used quotation was from *Coming to Our Senses: The Significance of the Arts for American Education*, published by the American Council for the Arts.

Two years previously, in June of 1976, Thomas Sly, Joseph Brockett, and Ronn Kistler had committed their professional lives to providing such "soul nourishment" in Huntington Station, New York. The three men had met as members of the arts-in-education company at the Performing Arts Foundation of Long Island (PAF). Under the inspired leadership of Clint Marantz, Kelly Patton, and Kas Bendiner, PAF had been, since its inception, in the vanguard of the arts-in-education movement.

Thomas, founder and president of Creative Educational Systems, was a businessman turned clown, teacher, artistic director of Long Island's first year-round professional theater for young people, associate producer, and director of research and development for PAF. Joseph, PAF's artistic director, was a professional actor, director, and playwright who had taught theater at Stanford and Northwestern Universities and had been co-producer of a professional children's theater company in New York City. Ronn was diverted from a career in biochemistry to become an actor-teacher and arts-in-education training director for PAF. All three participated in the growth of one of the nation's most acclaimed pioneering programs in the then new field of arts-in-education.

Sly, Brockett and Kistler shared a common vision: to make the visual and performing arts available as teaching strategies to all educators everywhere.

With a band of youngsters (several just out of high school) they formed CES as an arts-in-education consultation firm and began an intensive training session and period of research on how people learn, what participation in the arts teaches, and how all the arts may be used to communicate curriculum and behavioral objectives.

Within a year, they were presenting at state and regional conferences, doing workshops throughout the state of New York, and applying their techniques in schools, businesses, hospitals, youth organizations, theaters, churches, and government agencies.

Over the next five years, they expanded their services to California and Colorado, while maintaining corporate headquarters in New York. Video and film production followed, the reception by educators was enthusiastic, and they began organizing the documentation of their experiences to be shared with others.

In 1983, aware of the radical changes occurring in American education, the need for a deepening and broadening of their work became apparent. They curtailed their activities and went on sabbatical leave to the Teton Mountains in Wyoming for further study.

In 1989, CES moved to Southern California and began a series of in-service workshops for teachers and artist-in-residence programs in public schools. Much had changed in 15 years. The field of arts-in-education had expanded to become a department within the National Endowment for the Arts. Major granting organizations had set up arts-in-education programs in teacher training colleges throughout the country. The Kennedy Center for the Performing Arts in Washington, D.C., had established a National Alliance for Arts Education. More than ever before, educators were recognizing the value of the arts to the education of the whole child.

This book has been written in response to the eager and insightful questions of the thousands of teachers who have been inspired to see the possibilities of significantly integrating the arts into the educational process.

A creative educational system is a set of integrated, arts-based teaching strategies which involves the whole person: heart, mind, body, and soul. Such a system endows the participant with a sense of vision beyond the ordinary. It expands the imagination, and stimulates critical thinking. It stirs the emotions and encourages active participation in the learning process. Most important, it allows the individual to vitalize and express the creative spirit inherent in each of us through the magic of the visual and performing arts.

"One ought every day to hear a little song, read a good poem, see a fine picture and if possible, speak a few reasonable words."

Goethe

NIGHT LIGHT

With the formulation of any new
conceptual process,
comes a period of patience
during which the formula is
tested,
tried,
expanded and
contracted.
A period of waiting
through doubt and disbelief.
This period is often,
experientially,
a time of pain
and separation.
Some call it a time of darkness;
like a room--
a room of darkness
where one must grope
and stumble
with only memories of the door
to guide you.
When, at last,
through perseverance
and faith that the door was ever there,
you reach out
and you touch the handle,
the door slowly opens,
and a thin shaft of light
meets your eyes and
you thank God
your blindness is gone
and you can
go on.

WTS

TABLE OF CONTENTS

A Call for Unity of Purpose

In this time of global transition, when ethics and values, self-awareness and self-esteem are being recognized as the essence of conscious living, then we, as educators, must reappraise our responsibility in guiding the hearts and minds of our nation's youth. Our mission is not to bring music, drama, literature, or academic subjects to the children. Rather our mission is to bring <u>purpose</u> to education, to life itself.

Art is the clearest, purest mirror of the nature of Man. Art can be the prism which translates the clear, direct light of science and the humanities into the rainbow of education.

Since the dawn of recorded time, the arts have been used to in-struct (create an inner structure), to teach or lead, to educate, to draw out the creative understanding of every individual, of every group. We must now recognize that Art is not a diversion from Reality. Art is a reflection of Reality.

Artists have long been acknowledged as psychological <u>interpreters</u> of the times, demonstrating through their expressions, the barometer of Society's moods or dependencies and frustrations, or joys and victories. Let us then, as educators, join with artists to develop <u>creative</u> educational systems which will find and bring out, nurture and inspire the innate creativity of every child, so they may creatively respond to the world as they find it.

Let us approach our life on Earth as a level of experiential learning, a theatre of educational events; where we learn to use our intellect, guided by our heart, in alliance with will and wisdom. Let us plant seeds of giving, of sharing, of helping within the depths of our being. And let us then strive to grow into fulfillment of our highest aspirations. Let us rise above our apparent limitations and inspire the young souls who trust us to lead them.

One grows by helping others. One helps others by growing.

W Thomas Sly

12

CHAPTER ONE

WHAT IS
ARTS-IN-EDUCATION?

IMAGINE...

What if coming to school each morning were a joy for teachers and students alike? What if every classroom were a place of exhilaration and fresh wonder, each day a celebration, each teacher a fount of inspiration? What if every child expressed their highest potential in school ...and then ventured forth to build a better world?

What if an educational system might be devised through which every teacher were encouraged to use his or her special gifts to guide and motivate, to monitor, and to reveal the universe in which we live and move and have our being? What if the learning of every child was designed to discover and nurture that special individuality which each of us possesses?

Visions and dreams are what propel us forward in our eternal pursuit of truth and love and beauty. Every aspect of our civilization is the result of the visions and dreams of the past. What our world will become in the future will be the result of the visions and dreams we create now.

What a glorious opportunity we are given to awaken the minds, open the hearts, and strengthen the wills of the young people in our classrooms today who will become the citizens of the world tomorrow.

Are we up to the challenge of being visionaries? Can we construct our dreams so they may become realities? Are we willing to venture into the unknown, seeking the mysteries of a better life and a world which works for all its inhabitants? Are we willing to inspire our students to do the same?

How do we stimulate the creative urges of our students? How do we channel their abundant energy? How do we draw out of them the innate desire to become the brightest and best they can be? And how can we fan that flame of desire into a blaze of creative action throughout the days of their lives?

A century ago, John Ruskin wrote:

> *Great nations write their autobiographies in three manuscripts: the*
> *book of their deeds, the book of their words and the book of their*
> *art. Not one of these books can be understood unless we read the*
> *two others; but of the three, the only trustworthy one is the last.*

Why is this so? Why is art "the clearest, purest mirror of the nature of Man?" Might it be because the images we bring forth in works of art come from the deepest center of who we truly are? Is it because when we are in the act of creation our hearts, minds, and wills are engaged all at the same time? How can we better know ourselves than to express our essence? How can we be more true to ourselves than to take what is inside us and share it with one another?

And, as educators, what greater gift can we give our students than the opportunity to discover their wholeness?

Integrating the arts into the learning process educates the whole child.

"When the Artist is alive in any person, whatever his kind of work may be, he becomes an inventive, searching, daring, self expressive creature. He becomes interesting to other people. He disturbs, upsets, enlightens and opens ways for a better understanding."

Robert Henri
"The Art Spirit"

TURN ON THE LIGHT ☺

We all want to be loved, to love and have that love returned, to be acknowledged, to feel good about ourselves, to grow, in whatever ways we value.

We all like to be reminded that we are human, even students... even teachers. Whether we are more than that is something for our humanness to discover. But at the very least, we *are* humans... being.

We all think brilliant thoughts along with outrageous absurdities. Our emotions fluctuate from moment to moment, depending on such vagaries as the weather, the time of day, the flash of a color, a chance remark, or a wayward thought winging its way through our consciousness. Our bodies are uncomfortable a good deal of the time. We're generally very attached to our opinions, even while convincing ourselves we are free and open-minded. Our moods and attitudes shift and dissolve like waves on the ocean and we mostly spend our lives doing a never-ending juggling act between freedom and responsibility, fulfillment and futility, boredom and excitement. In these respects, we are just like... everyone else!

One of the qualities of being human appears to be a reluctant resistance to change. We will stoutly maintain we support progress and, at the same time, freeze up if it means we must change a comfortable pattern.

Realistically, are we *afraid?* Of what? Of being uncomfortable again as we were before we established our "comfortable pattern?" Sometimes, we're fortunate enough to hide our fear from ourselves by calling it "excitement" (same thing as fear, really, depending on your point of view). And in those instances, our shift from one paradigm into another becomes adventure rather than trauma. As teachers, it may help us to remember a student confronts this potential challenge upon entering every classroom.

And as students... of the unfolding drama of Life, it may help us to remember that everything and everyone is our teacher. Some courses of learning in "Life's schoolroom" are required, some elective. Some teachers are wise and compassionate. Some are severe and unfair. Some are foolish and full of themselves. They're all effective, however, in helping us to learn about ourselves and our universe. Over time... we learn and grow and become more fully ourselves.

Arts-in-education is merely the recognition and appreciation of an element in education that has always been there, inherent in human nature. Of course, we respond to color and light, sound and movement, just as surely as we respond to ideas and emotions. Those sensory and emotional, sometimes kinetic experiences we call "the arts" are a treasure in the process of learning. Such a simple, natural, human function as creative expression must necessarily, by its nature, expand our perspective, help us humans to *be* more completely, to grow... to learn.

Consciously using all the visual and performing arts as learning tools is effective, important, easy, fun, challenging, a little scary, and worth whatever effort it takes to do it successfully.

When you see that light go on behind a student's eyes, it makes it all worthwhile, doesn't it?

What follows is a distillation of techniques, strategies, concepts, and suggestions that we of Creative Educational Systems have seen "turn on the light' in thousands of classrooms across the country over the past twenty years.

ARTISTS AT HEART ♥

Imagination.   The image nation.   I, mage.

What a wealth of images travel through the universe of our minds! And what joy we feel when we can grasp a favored image and bring it into our world of the senses. Watch any child drawing a picture, making a May basket out of construction paper, or modeling a candy dish out of clay. And compare the light of concentrated rapture in their eyes with that in the eyes of a master painter at work. Or sculptor or poet. The look is the same, albeit tempered and mellowed with skill, experience, and wisdom in the older artist.

We are all artists at heart, if not in mind. We all yearn to express our most intense feelings... and do so, though not always in a form which can be accepted by the world as "art." All of us experience joy in expressing our feelings to the degree our feelings are joyous. And the more self-confidence we have in expressing, and the more sublime the image we choose to bring forth, the more joy we feel.

All teachers are artists. Yes, teaching is a science *and* it is also an art. Artists are those who focus the bulk of their energies on expressing their deepest, highest, most precious feelings. And if we don't all feel deeply about teaching, what on earth would keep us in the profession? Certainly not the high pay, prestige, easy hours, or glamourous lifestyle!

All teachers are artists. And all artists are teachers. The mirrors artists create teach us again and again who we are, both individually and collectively. The difference between "teacher" and "artist" is a matter of form. Arts-in-education is a union of complements, the blending of art forms, each becoming enriched in the process.

A DEFINITION OF ARTS-IN-EDUCATION

"Arts-in-education" is the name given to the use of the visual and performing arts to teach, to convey information. All arts are vehicles for communication. They are as effective in many instances (and more effective in others) as any textbook, lecture, workbook, or other traditional method used in the classroom.

In addition to the content of a particular piece, the visual arts may communicate principles of balance, composition, and individual style. Music can communicate much about ethnic cultures, the motivations of human passions, and the rhythms of life itself. Dance both celebrates and informs us about the complexities of the human body and the concept of spatial relationships.

Drama, especially, is an effective tool for learning, as it combines physicalization with emotional and sensory awareness of intellectual experience. Students learn on many planes simultaneously. They are learning through right-brain, as well as left-brain, experiences.

The concept of integrating the performing arts into the classroom may cause some apprehension at first, until we realize, in the words of William Shakespeare, "All the world's a stage and all the men and women merely players...," even teachers and students.

We are already using all the elements of the theater in our daily lives anyway. Why not just be aware of (and consciously *use)* costuming, sets, props, lights and sound to create the kind of mood we wish to have in the classroom on any given day, for any given lesson?

How will we know what costume is right, or which piece of music will inspire the right feeling for the lesson? We will learn through allowing both our experience and our intuition to be our guides. Perhaps we, as well as our children, already have within us the knowledge we need to make our lives rich and full... it merely needs to be drawn forth (educated).

> *"Our goal is not to make every student an artist, but to exploit art as an unique vehicle for developing the individual creative potential in every student. As an open-ended, unrestricted context for thinking and caring, art expands our capacity to perceive, understand, and appreciate life. Limited only by the power of our imaginations, art confronts the unknown and attempts the impossible in order to construct new meanings. Art exalts the best and the most that human beings can be: it inspires us to surpass ourselves."*

Jon J. Murray

READY, GET SET...

We have to know where to start. If we're going to integrate the arts into the educational system, we have to know why we are doing it, that we are indeed capable of doing it, and a few basic ground rules. That's what we will cover in this chapter.

In successive chapters, we will find out the "How." How to do everything from making a simple theater game work in our classroom, to teaching our entire curriculum through the arts, to mounting a theatrical production.

Core literature, historical events or cultural/ethical concepts may easily and effectively be approached through the use of the arts. Stories, incidents or concepts can be acted out. They can be illustrated. They can be pantomimed and moved to music. They can be sung or expressed through sound. And, by expressing ourselves through various art forms, we not only allow for an intellectual understanding of the material, we also encourage an emotional, physical, and sensory understanding as well.

STRETCHING THE IMAGE

"Wisdom: the quality of being wise; power of judging rightly and following the soundest course of action, based on knowledge, experience, understanding, etc."

Wisdom is a quality of mind and heart sought by many and acquired only through time and experience. It is the ultimate goal and purpose of education. Wisdom is not easy to teach, but one thing is certain. To be wise, one cannot rely on facts alone. One must delve into the world of meaning. A start in this direction can perhaps be made by teaching students to look beyond the obvious, to search for meanings, to "stretch the image."

☺ *ACTIVITY: THE STICK GAME.* Start with a simple image like a yardstick or pointer, the simple physicalization of a straight line. That's an image which can be stretched through acting. What can you make the stick into? A pogo stick? A flute? A toothbrush? Act them out. Treat the stick as though it were the object you imagine, and the "audience" (the class) members will respond accordingly. They will stretch the image. (For variations, see *Stick Game*, p.36).

☺ *ACTIVITY: FREE ASSOCIATION.* Using a word like "joy," stretch the image by free associating with picture words which make you feel joy - like "rainbow," "roses," or "pizza."

Activities like these are simple ways to get students to make connections, to take a concept and expand it and apply it to a different set of imaginary conditions, to stretch the image. In so doing, they set up a mental pattern which will help them, over time, develop the ability to see different points of view, to recognize the meaning behind the facts they learn, to make choices based on understanding their options... to acquire wisdom.

This book contains a wealth of activities and information. Many of the activities herein are adapted from other sources for use in the classroom. Take whatever concepts, activities, and games you know or find in this book and stretch them. Apply them for different purposes, vary them, restructure them. As you practice, you will begin to think like an artist, to make connections, to creatively problem solve. And you will fill your own and your students' lives with rainbows, roses, and pizza. ☺

"I look forward to a world which is not afraid of grace and beauty."

John F. Kennedy

CREATIVITY AND CHAOS IN THE CLASSROOM

The way to control the chaos unleashed by right-brain creativity is to use left-brain organizational skills to channel all that energy into a desired direction.

Few things in most lives are more chaotic than a play in the last stages of rehearsal; than setting up a scene in a film studio before the cameras start rolling; than an artist's or musician's or writer's studio during moments of inspiration and creation.

Why? For the simple reason that the creator's focus has narrowed to exclude virtually everything other than the work he or she is producing. This is equally true in the classroom when real creativity is happening.

The *trick* of controlling it all is first to have an *objective*. Early in the creative process, the artist needs to have some concept of a finished product - how it will look, sound, or feel.

A good objective will tell you *what* it is you're going to do; *how* it is to be done (if you're going to put on a play, are you going to use a published script, write a script yourselves, or create it improvisationally?); *when* it is to be completed (the essay will be due Monday, the play will be performed on Halloween, the project will be completed by the end of the quarter, etc.); *where* it will happen (in class? at home? in the all-purpose room?); *who* will do it (the whole class? a special group of students?).

You may be wondering what happened to *why!* Rest assured that consideration of the skills involved in accomplishing the "what," "how," "when," "where," and "who" will usually reveal the "why" with crystal clarity.

Once you have your objective, you need a *schedule* of steps toward accomplishment. The structure of a Rehearsal Schedule for a play is a workable model for this. **When making up such a schedule, you always start at the end and work your way back to the beginning.** (See *Rehearsal Schedule*, p.106).

A schedule will help keep you and your students on track. And it is most important that the schedule be designed with built-in flexibility. Some things take more or less time than estimated. The unexpected can be expected. Sometimes a "miracle" occurs. A play suddenly comes together. Colors blend magically. Harmonies surprise. The turn of a phrase illuminates. Creativity provides fertile ground for inspiration.

Chaos is merely energy in an unformed state. Don't be afraid of it, even though it may temporarily upset a comfortable, proven routine. Rather, learn to control it and shape it to a desired end.

The arts are a risky business. They can transform the mundane into the sublime. And in the classroom, as in life, some risks are worth taking.

ACCOMPLISHMENT SCHEDULE FORM - SAMPLE

Objective: Ms. Lee's fifth grade class will put on an original dramatic version of "Puebla Battle Day" on the fifth of May (Cinquo de Mayo) in the school cafeteria.

What: A dramatization of "Puebla Battle Day."

How: Original (the class will make up the play themselves).

When: May 5, 10 a.m.

Where: School Cafeteria, playing in the round.

Who: Ms. Lee's fifth grade class, assisted by parents, volunteers, aides, and teacher.

Why: Self Confidence
Oral Expression
Kinesthetic Movement
An understanding of the story of "Puebla Battle Day"
An understanding of Cinco de Mayo
Dramatic involvement
Developing creativity
Understanding how to write a play
etc.

ACCOMPLISHMENT SCHEDULE FORM - REPRODUCIBLE

Objective:

What:

How:

When:

Where:

Who:

Why:

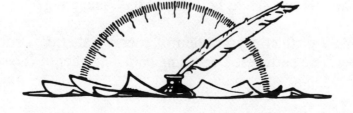

ENERGY - KEY TO SUCCESS

Webster defines "energy" as potential force, inherent power, and the capacity for vigorous action. The learning process is an exchange of energy between students and teachers.

Teach your students about energy as an *interactive* force and you will experience benefits in many areas. Your students' understanding of how energy works will positively affect the class discipline and will help to focus your class for the rest of the year, as well as focusing each student's own self-awareness for the rest of their lives.

HOW DOES ENERGY WORK?

All Being is action,
And all action is energy
And all energy is reciprocal
in exchange
and therefore
you feel a wall
or rather
there is a reciprocity
of energy
between you and the wall
and verification of that spiritual experience
on the physical plane
comes when you touch with your hand,
the wall...

Excerpt from "A Simple Thread of Reality"
WTS

Energy is the life force. It is the basic building block for the universe.

☺ *ACTIVITY: BASIC BUILDING BLOCKS.* Pick an object in the room, a chair, for instance. Discuss what the chair is made of. You may get "wood and metal." Ask students to break it down further: What is wood made of? "Fibers." And what makes up fibers? "Molecules." And molecules are made of...? "Atoms." And the atoms...? Eventually you get back to the level of "energy," organized in a particular pattern to create sub-atomic particles.
Pick another object, e.g., a wall. You can go through the same discussion and discover the wall, too, is made of energy.
A person? Made of energy.
Discuss how this is possible. How can something as solid and immovable as a wall, something like a chair which we can pick up and move around, and a complex human being who can talk and think, be made of the same thing?

Each entity is a distinct organization of energy patterns. Different patterns of energy create different sub-atomic particles. Depending on the number of each of these, different kinds of atoms are created. There are approximately 100 different kind of atoms, some "created" by man. These 100 or so different energy patterns can be combined in myriad combinations to form molecules. And so forth up the complexity chain to larger and larger numbers of possible combinations of energy patterns. At least in the animal kingdom, molecules make tissues, which make organs, which make organisms.

One can now get a glimpse of the marvelous complexity of a human being as an intricate pattern of energy, and why it took mankind so long to evolve.

EMOTIONS AS ENERGY

Stretch the concept of energy beyond its usual boundaries. What is air made of? Energy. And sound? Energy. Light? Energy.

What about emotions? The answer must, after some thought, be energy. Hmm. Could it be that all those feelings we call "anger" or "sorrow" or even "love" are merely labeled forms of energy? Is it possible we might be able to control them? Even change them at will?

☺ **TOPIC FOR DISCUSSION: ENERGY TRANSFER.** Ask your students: "Have you ever been in a situation where someone comes along in a really bad mood (i.e., they're experiencing a "negative" emotion - anger, fear, guilt, etc.); all of a sudden, for no apparent reason, you're in a bad mood too? Why?"

The opposite scenario is also possible. A person who is radiating good feelings can come into a room of gloomy or bored people and, by sheer dint of his or her positive emotional energy level, get everyone else feeling good too.

Husbands and wives, or any two very close people, will recognize this happening between them frequently. Why? Because they have made themselves vulnerable to each other, which means they are receptive to each other's emotional energy.

So emotions, too, are energy and, yes, we can control them. Emotions don't just happen to us. We (frequently unconsciously) choose what we feel. And theater is a marvelous tool for learning to make choices conscious. We can learn conscious control of our emotions.

☺ **ACTIVITY: CONTROLLING EMOTIONS.** Have students role-play an emotional situation, e.g., one student asks another for a crayon (ruler, textbook) and the first student won't give it up. Have them do the improvisation with different emotional endings, e.g., the students get angry at each other, the students compromise and share, the students get a third party to arbitrate. Have the class offer as many options to end the scene as they can think of, and let the actors play each one.

By improvising, they will be guided into a thought pattern and perspective which allows them to play out any given emotional choice. For example, to get angry as a result of the crayon incident, they will have to take a perspective on the situation and think thoughts which will ultimately make them angry. Should they encounter this kind of situation in real life, they now know the perspective they adopt and the thought pattern they follow to achieve an angry ending.

Once they've acted out various alternative endings, they will be better able to recognize their own reactions in a real-life situation and choose the perspective and thoughts which will give them the result they want.

THOUGHTS AS ENERGY

What about thoughts? Are thoughts energy too? Buckminster Fuller (reknowned scientist, engineer, and futurist) believed such was the case. It would certainly make sense. Otherwise, how can some people suddenly know something has happened to a loved one miles away? You may have a close friend whose thoughts you sometimes know without asking.

Fuller coined the term "synchronicity" to describe the phenomenon of two or more people coming up with the same idea at the same time in different areas of the world. They had "tuned in," Fuller believed, to the same frequency of thought energy. How can two people sit in separate rooms, without conferring, and end up drawing the same picture? Some people can do this. It might be interesting to try this activity with your students:

☺ *ACTIVITY: THOUGHT TRANSFER*. Send two students to separate and isolated, quiet areas. Have them sit quietly for several minutes, not thinking of anything in particular, just listening to sounds around them. After two minutes of quiet, they should try to make their minds blank. Let one student, chosen previously, draw something simple, keeping this image as strongly in mind as possible. Let the other student allow images to come to mind, and draw the one which seems the strongest. Compare the results after about five minutes, or whenever they feel they are finished. Is there any relationship between the two pictures?

Many students will not be able (at least initially) to connect with others' thoughts at all. But you will find occasional combinations of students who tune in to each other surprisingly well. They may not always draw exactly the same image, but there may be some relationship, indicating some level of thought connection, e.g., one student may draw a crescent moon and another may draw a banana. This activity is fun and interesting and will help students to more clearly relate to thoughts as energy.

CHANGES IN ENERGY

After a basic understanding of energy and how it functions has been achieved, your class will be ready to study the *focusing* of energy. Play some of the sense awareness games (see p.42). They will then be receptive to changes in energy and ready to try the following activities.

☺ *ACTIVITY: MOOD CHANGES*. Have students sit quietly and feel the difference in energy ("mood" might be a more easily grasped concept) between different styles of music. Try different sounds, too, including silence. Have students give an image for the kind of energy each sound feels like, e.g., cloud, circus, loneliness, fireworks.
Repeat the activity using different qualities of light to change the mood, e.g., candlelight, lamplight, colored light. Let your students try on different costumes and different hairstyles and look at themselves in a mirror. Then let them give you their impressions of the qualities of energy of the different characters they have assumed, e.g., fiery, lazy, moody, nervous, etc.

FOCUSING ENERGY

☺   *ACTIVITY: ENERGY FOCUS*. Divide the group in half, "actors" and "audience." Have the actors go on stage (to the front of the class). Assign each actor a different number. Have them walk around the space in a random pattern, not talking, not touching, nor relating to one another. Call out one of their numbers.

When a student's number is called, they are to stay essentially where they are, but briefly adjust their body position, if necessary, so as to become the focus of attention in the "scene." All other actors are to stay essentially where they are, but adjust their body positions only as much as necessary to give focus to the person whose number was called. After the slight adjustment has been made, the actors *must* freeze. This is important. They must hold this frozen picture while the audience evaluates the stage picture. It is important to realize (and should be obvious to the audience) even the slightest movement from an actor can change the focus and thus the stage picture, or pattern of spatial relationships.

Example: Ten students are milling around on stage. The director calls "Five." Actor Five throws his arms up in the air and freezes. Other actors turn their heads toward Actor Five, and freeze.

Evaluation: Ask the audience if actors achieved the objective? Which actor has the focus? Is it Five? Are all others giving focus? Is there a split focus? How is Five taking focus? What is he doing to accomplish the objective?

It will soon become apparent that there are many ways to get focus. (Incidentally, though sound and motion are good focus takers, they should be eliminated at first from this activity so students can understand physical focus). If the audience is not convinced the objective has been achieved, ask them to suggest the tiniest adjustment which will achieve it. Actors should move only at the command of the teacher, e.g., when it is pointed out that Actor Three is also taking focus, Three may tend to react physically to the news by moving, thereby destroying the picture the audience was working on. The audience should be made aware of this. After all actors' numbers have been called, have actors and audience switch roles. Repeat the activity.

✓   **TIP:** You may find you prefer to precede this stage focus activity by using a painting to help students identify the focus of a picture, i.e., where their eyes tend to go.

☺   *ACTIVITY: FOCUS WITH STAGE PICTURE*. Repeat the same activity, but have actors work not only for focus, but also for an interesting stage picture or composition. Again you may wish to precede this activity by using a painting to demonstrate composition.

Example: In the previous activity, Five is stage center with his hands in the air. Other actors are lined up on either side of Five, evenly spaced, with hands at their sides, all facing front with their bodies, and with their heads turned toward Five. This will achieve the focus of energy, but is it as interesting to look at as the next example?

Example: Five is stage center with hands in the air. Three actors are grouped closely together in the upstage right corner (see *Stage Areas*, p.96). Two actors are on the same line as Five, closer to him, but are grouped closely together and are both down on one knee. Three actors are in the downstage left corner; two of them have their arms around each other's shoulder and the third is sitting on the ground with her legs stretched out towards Five. Two other actors are slightly upstage and left of Five, the front one with her hands on her knees, slightly crouched, and the back one leaning on the front one. All are looking at Five.

Evaluation: Which of the two examples is more interesting to look at? Is any actor blocking another actor's face? What is the least amount of adjustment which can be made in the scene to strengthen the focus? to make the picture more interesting? to avoid a block? to give a more balanced feeling?

Obviously, evaluation of the stage picture gets into the subjective area of taste and preference. But awareness of picture will improve the visual aspects of any performance, whether theatrical, musical, or dance. It will also improve visual art displays, e.g., what is the most interesting arrangement of student paintings displayed on the school's wall? All in rows? In groupings? Is the wall, as a whole work of art, balanced and interesting to look at?

In evaluating stage picture, consider the elements of creativity (see p.48) to see how many are being utilized effectively.

FOCUS BY PERSONAL ENERGY ALONE

☺   *ACTIVITY: PROJECTING CHARISMA.* Have two students stand on stage, sharing the focus, turned at quarter position toward each other (see *Blocking*, p.95). The teacher calls out one student's name, then the other's. Each student, as he is called, increases his or her energy output, taking focus by exuding energy alone. Imagining themselves as strong, confident and enthusiastic, or picturing themselves as a light bulb getting brighter or as forcing out energy in all directions, may be useful images to accomplish this task. The other student drops his or her energy level, giving focus. Imagining themselves as small and receptive to everything, including energy, may help. What energy the second actor does exude should be directed toward the first actor. Neither should shift their body position, except in response to energy exuded.

Ask the audience members if they can see a shift in focus. If they can see this as an audience and accomplish it as actors, they should be able to focus their energy at will. If a class's attention wanders, calling "Focus!" should be enough to put them back on task.

You will find some students are excellent at giving you focus, energy, and support. These are the ones whose energy you need when you are trying to make an important point. Others, of course, tend to take more energy than they give. The more focused the class's energy, the more complete the learning moment. The same principle, spoken to an unfocused class, will not have nearly the impact or be as readily retained as when spoken with forcefulness and energy to a focused class. The best results are achieved when the teacher consciously takes focus and the class consciously gives focus.

FAILURE AND SUCCESS

"Know thyself."
Socrates

"To thine own self be true."
William Shakespeare

Someone very wise has said, "The only failure is giving up."

From time to time, gentle and compassionate teachers have expressed hesitancy about involving students in the performing arts because they fear an unsuccessful experience might damage a student's self-esteem. That's possible. Failure to pass an important test might do the same thing. A gift rejected, a relationship broken, a dream thwarted... each of these may cause any of us to pause and reconsider who we are, regardless of our age or level of maturity.

Buckminster Fuller failed at everything he tried for forty years and was on the verge of suicide until he decided to try one more time and discovered his destiny. Albert Einstein was a poor student in school, his teachers declaring he was a hopeless dreamer and probably wouldn't amount to very much. Thomas Edison was considered "slow."

Every one of us has failed at one thing or another in our life. And what has been the result? Well, we have "pulled ourselves up by the bootstraps" and gone on. Life is about living, after all. It's a *process*, and a necessary part of that process is experimentation.

Forgetting one's lines during a performance, not speaking loudly enough to be heard by the audience, delivering a comedy punchline which falls flat - none of these is any more or less traumatic than missing a basket in the last quarter of the big game, or breaking out with a pimple on the end of your nose on the night of the prom!

Certainly positive self-esteem ranks high on the list of those qualities which make for a healthy, well-balanced life. As educators, it is undeniably our responsibility to do our utmost to foster self-awareness, self-esteem and self-confidence in each and every one of our students (*and in ourselves as well*). This cannot be achieved in any lasting sense, however, by overprotecting our charges from the realities of active participation in the creative expression of their uniqueness. Rather, when students discover who they truly are by testing their mettle in all sorts of experiences, they can make choices for success with strength and surety.

Education is not a spectator sport.

A "wise old owl" in a Walt Disney movie once sang:

"It's what you do with what you've got
And never mind how much you've got,
It's what you do with what you got
That matters in the end!" ♥

Press On

Nothing in the world can take the place of persistence.
Talent will not;
Nothing is more common than unsuccessful individuals with talent.
Genius will not;
Unrewarded genius is almost a proverb.
Education will not;
The world is full of educated derelicts.
Persistence and determination alone are omnipotent.

Anonymous ☺

CHAPTER TWO

CREATIVE DRAMA

"It is the supreme art of the teacher to awaken joy in creative expression and knowledge."

Albert Einstein

Creative drama is a first step in nurturing and expanding the student's imagination, turning daydreams into goals, and revealing a universe of possibilities.

The root word of "create" means "to grow." The origin of the word "drama" is a Greek word meaning "to do." Thus, one could say, semantically, creative drama is "to grow by doing."

It is the imagination which grows through creative drama. And there is no faculty of the mind more important in building a life than the imagination. Without it, we would all be mere automatons, acting solely on the basis of observable facts, following orders rather than making choices, leading dry, empty lives rather than rich, colorful ones.

The basic premise of arts-in-education is that through the nurturing of a rich imagination and the wise application of its harvest, each of us can create a life which is fulfilling for ourselves and of benefit to others.

"Lift up your hearts
Each new hour holds new chances
For new beginnings."

Maya Angelou

IMPROVISATION

Improvisation is "making it up as you go."

Improvisation is what we all do all the time, every day of our lives. We never know exactly what we may encounter or what someone may say to us, let alone how we will react, so we improvise from moment to moment.

Improvisation is an excellent way to start young people acting. It motivates them to focus on meaning and sequences of events, rather than a rote memorizing of other people's words.

Script work is valid and an important part of a student's dramatic literacy, but often beginning students are able to get out of a scripted play only a monotonous recitation. With improvisation, honesty takes care of itself, because the students are responding spontaneously.

Speed is another advantage of improvisation (improv). Just tell a class a story, assign characters, and go! Though the first run-through may be unpolished (depending on the experience of your student actors), in one class period you will have created a play in rough form. Sometimes it will even be good enough to show another class that same day. Let the class decide.

Improvisational drama teaches critical thinking, spontaneous creativity, and physical and oral expression.

WARMING UP

When preparing to act something out with a class, whether scripted or improvised, it is helpful to warm them up with one or more theater games. The games listed later (p. 34) provide good warm-ups and achieve several other objectives at the same time. These games are to actors what barre exercises are to dancers, what scales are to musicians, or what lay-up drills are to basketball players. They may be played again and again with benefit, regardless of the age or level of experience of the actors. They are also a great way to introduce youngsters to creative drama.

For older children, improvisation will loosen them up and help them to overcome self-consciousness. The games also encourage them to become actively involved because "it's fun!" After students of the fourth grade and above have gained a little confidence in improvisation, assigning them roles to play in an actual production will seem like a reward for participating.

Students can be taught a reasonable degree of sophistication in improvisation through theater games. Look up the section on theater games (p.34) and start your students with games like Non-Stop Talking (p.34) and Tennis Ball (p.36), followed by Parts of a Whole (p.37).

IMPROVISING SCENES

With children in the primary grades, it is probably best to start out by narrating a story and have the children act out the various characters as you get to them. Usually, enough parts can be found to have each child play a role. If necessary, however, break the story into different scenes and have the same role played by several different children at different times. In improvisational theater, anything can be a character: trees, animals, wind, even abstract qualities like "fear" and "love."

Then, especially for third grade and above, break them into groups and assign improvs to each group. For instance:

☺   *ACTIVITY: BASIC IMPROV.* Have each group pick a favorite nursery rhyme, or fairy tale and act it out. Give them 5-10 minutes to plan their improvisation, and then let the whole class watch each group's scene. In introducing the activity, emphasize "beginning, middle, and end" and "characters" in each scene. Watch to make sure they include these things. If they are successful, their improvisations should be quite theatrical.

Next, give them each an historical event to improvise. Then let them create a scene communicating a message about using drugs, or conserving energy, or preserving the environment, or any objective you've been working on in class.

Two basic questions to ask students about their improvs are, "Can the audience *hear* everything?" and "Can the audience *see* everything?" If not, try a *Projection Exercise* (p.92) or go over basic blocking principles with them (p.100).

☺   *ACTIVITY: IMAGE IMPROVS.* As your class gets better, give them less structured starting places for their improvs: a picture, a line of poetry, or a quotation, as examples. Have them make the connection between what you've given them and something in their own lives through an improvisation. For example, if one group gets a picture of a water tower, they might choose to do an improvisation on conserving water.

This exercise in making connections will stimulate their imaginations and creativity, while preparing them for more advanced activities.

GETTING THEM "PSYCHED" TO IMPROVISE A PLAY

Tell or read them the story. Get them to discuss it. Ask them how they think one character or another *felt* about a particular incident in the story. *The expression of feelings is important in the acting out of any story.* Discuss the clothes they think the characters might have worn, or what they looked like. Get them to come up with as many sensory images as possible about the setting and, if applicable, the historical period. Stimulate their imaginations by using yours.

MAKING THE PLAY

After you have assigned roles, break the story up into different scenes. Most stories take place in several different locations and at several different times. Each setting may involve different characters.

Work on each scene individually. Guide the students through the scene, but allow them to say and do whatever they like, as long as they don't stray too far from the meaning of the scene. *Emphasize that there is no "right" or "wrong" in theater.* Either the actors communicate the story to the audience, or they don't.

Communication is the key concept.

Make sure you assign a particular area of the room (or stage) for each character in each scene, so the students will not be insecure as to where to stand or sit.

Also, make sure your students know when to start a scene and when to end it. Give them a "cue" to enter: perhaps a line of narration, a specific line of dialogue, a particular action on stage or a special piece of music.

One effective way for an improvisational scene to end is to have the characters "freeze" for a moment before exiting. Or, if it fits into the story, a simple exit by those in a scene will, of course, suffice.

REHEARSING

After each scene is worked out, it's time to put all the scenes together and practice them in sequence. This can be where *your* creativity gets a chance to express itself!

Encourage students to speak loudly and clearly enough to be heard and understood, to stand still until they have someplace to go, and (generally) to look at whoever on stage is speaking.

Help them, if they need it, to *show* the emotions of the characters. Shaking a fist or stomping a foot if angry, bowing the head if sorrowful, walking on tiptoes and peering over one's shoulders if fearful are simple actions which can add color and drama to the situation and help the players become even more involved.

After each rehearsal, have the students give themselves a hand. Applause will make them feel good about what they have done, and eager to do more. After two or three rehearsals (depending on the complexity of the piece), they should be ready to share what they are doing with another class.

COSTUMES, PROPS, SCENERY, SOUND AND LIGHTS

These production elements are not really necessary to effective playmaking, but they do add a special theatricality to the situation.

Costumes may include simple masks or headdresses made in class, costume jewelry and discards from home, or particular items from the child's own wardrobe (like a party dress, or ragged blue jeans, or a white shirt, etc.).

Props (stage properties) may be anything from paper cups as goblets, a chair with a cloth draped over it for a throne, to a couple of sticks tied together to form a sword. A can of gold or silver spray paint can do wonders with pieces of hardware, walnut shells, or artificial flowers. And it's far more valuable for children to create their stage reality than to have it provided for them... It's imagination time again!

Scenery may be a picture drawn on the blackboard with colored chalk, a painted backdrop on brown wrapping paper, or cardboard cutouts of trees and shrubbery.

Turning out some or all of the lights in the room can be effective, as can bringing a table lamp or two from home and/or using colored light bulbs.

Appropriate music on cassette tape will contribute greatly to the mood of the piece; or perhaps children not on stage may play on simple rhythm instruments at different points in the story.

However simply or elaborately you prepare for the performance, involve the children as much as possible in the preparation. Use whatever's available... and make it fun. Playmaking should be an event, a special occasion, a spontaneous celebration. And have fun with it yourself! That's why they call it a "play!" ☺

PERFORMANCE

Primary children are delighted to perform for themselves. In grades three and above, however, the children are more likely to be thrilled by the experience if they have an audience-- another class, parents, even the whole school. And you'll enjoy it, too, *if* you always remember, *"the audience doesn't know what's supposed to happen!"*

♥ *Enjoy!* ☺

"Children are the living messages that we send to a time we will not see. They are a reflection of our culture."

Anonymous

The following games can be used as warm-ups before acting, or for specific curriculum objectives, if varied somewhat in format. Remember, when playing a game or leading an experience, you will have to find your own style. You will never be able to copy how someone else has led the activity. You will always have to make it your own.

♪ *NOTE:* Most theater games can be played with any age group, though the format may need to be varied or another game may be required as a warmup.

☺   *ACTIVITY: HELLO GAME.* Bouncing continuously on the balls of their feet, students talk non-stop to each other, moving around the room shaking as many hands as possible and saying "hello" and all sorts of nice things. On a pre-arranged signal, they continue to bounce, but they say grumbling, complaining, unpleasant things. On a final signal, they stop. This activity raises and directs energy, allows students to express their feelings in a non-threatening manner, and prepares them for the next directed activity.

☺   *ACTIVITY: NON-STOP TALKING.* The class is given a topic, e.g., "Peanut Butter," and, on a signal, they all have to talk about it simultaneously--non-stop. It doesn't matter if they speak utter nonsense, as long as they keep words coming out.

Variation: Different Subject Non-Stop. Each student non-stop talks on a different subject, everyone talking at once.

Variation: Non-Stop Argument. Pairs have non-stop talking arguments, e.g., one person thinks dogs are great, one doesn't. Both talk simultaneously to each other, non-stop. At first, all pairs go at once. Then individually. At a signal, they switch points-of-view and keep talking.

♪ *NOTE*: It is not important that students make an attempt to listen to each other, only that they talk non-stop.

Variation: Individual Non-Stop. Individuals non-stop talk by themselves.

Variation: Non-Stop Chorus. Each member has his or her own topic. The teacher conducts, directing chorus members to become louder or softer, cutting some voices out and bringing others in, rising to a crescendo and then bringing them to total silence.

♪ *NOTE:* After non-stop talking, students will be unable to justify "not knowing what to say" during improvisation.

☺   *ACTIVITY: MIRROR GAME.* Facing each other in pairs, sitting or standing, students silently behave as mirrors. One leads, the other tries to be an exact image. This must be done silently, with continuous eye contact, and in slow motion. After a while, call "switch." Without stopping the flow of the slow motion, the leaders become followers

34

(mirrors) and the followers start leading. After a few switches, call "eliminate the leader." They are then to follow each other simultaneously.

Variation: Group Mirrors. Once students become adept at mirroring one another with no leader, coach them to move, as mirrors, still playing the game, to join slowly with another group of mirrors. Then all four are to focus in the center of the group, with no leader, and try to follow each other. Keep joining the groups until the whole class is eventually in a circle--one large mirror game together.

Variation: Mirror Extension. While students are playing the mirror game in pairs, with no leader, let them know to keep playing with their partner while you move them around. You then slowly move one pair so that it is mirroring across another pair of mirrors. Each pair is to ignore the mirroring of the other pair and just mirror their partner; but, once they are all in place, coach them to be aware of the way space is formed by their movements. Ask them to be aware of images that come to mind, e.g., waterfall, ocean, rainbow. Bring the game to a close in silence and ask each person, without any other talking, to give you a one word image, perhaps something that came to mind while they were engaged in the activity. Write the images down and use them for a *Word Poem* (see p.41). This is an excellent activity for introducing poetry.

Mirror activities teach students focus, concentration, and getting in touch with each other on a non-verbal level.

☺ *ACTIVITY: STATUES*. Call out image words. The students silently and individually (but all at the same time) make statues of the words with their bodies. Start with strong, graphic images (emotions are usually good choices) and then move to easily identifiable objects, e.g., pumpkin, tree, airplane. Move into more abstract images such as "the color red," "freedom," or "yesterday."

Variation: Group Statues. Students may also make group statues. The whole group is to make the image you call out. If you say "tree," they are to make one tree out of five people, not five separate trees. Start with simple graphic images which are easy to create together, e.g., ball, house. Later they can act out more complex words or phrases such as a working sewing machine, an airplane, the city of New York, ancient Egypt, etc. Throughout this activity, they are to work silently and avoid the temptation to direct each other in the creation of the statue.

♪ *NOTE:* The above statue games place no emphasis on right or wrong appearance, simply on physical expression: it doesn't matter if a student makes a statue of a lollipop or of someone eating a lollipop, or if the statue looks nothing like a lollipop. It is only important that the student use his or her entire body in making the statue.

Variation: Graphics. Working in groups, students are secretly assigned an image and given one minute to prepare to act it out, as realistically as they can. Each group shows their image to the rest of the class. Once they have mastered this game, students will realize anything can become a character in a play, even inanimate objects. (Characters in "The Little Red Hen," might include--in addition to the animals--stalks of wheat, loaves of bread, a mill, an oven, etc.) This is a great way to make scenery, and to change quickly from one setting to the next.

♪ *NOTE:* Statues and graphics help students to get used to using their bodies to communicate, a very important part of acting.

☺   *ACTIVITY: TENNIS BALL.* With a partner, students engage in verbal persuasion. One partner has an imaginary tennis ball and the other partner tries to *talk* him out of it. It is important to emphasize the objective of each partner before starting; the one tries to get the ball, the other gives it to him *only* if he is satisfied with the reason. After a minute or two, have partners switch roles and play the game again. Whether or not they achieved their objective, students will be interested in discussing the various strategies they used.

Variation: Curriculum Ice Breaker. Use a curriculum topic which can be argued from different points of view, e.g., whether colonists should or should not revolt against England. One partner plays England and the other plays America trying to talk England into giving America independence.

♪ *NOTE:* This game works with most ages, and is especially good as an "ice-breaker" for older students. It demonstrates to students of any age that "anyone can act." Communicating verbally and with gestures, pursuing a specific objective, and using emotional appeals, together constitute the essence of acting.

☺   *ACTIVITY: NAME GAME.* Stand with the class in a circle. Students in turn say their names, each with a particular feeling and gesture. The class tries to immediately mimic each person, both by saying the name with the same inflection, and by making the same movements. Go on to the next person immediately. Do not allow students to pause to think, but encourage them to respond instantly and spontaneously. Good for any age.

Variation: Animal Name Game. Have the students say the name of an animal with an accompanying animal-like movement. The class mimics as before. This is a good preparation for acting out animals in an animal story.

♪ *NOTE:* It is wise to stipulate in both these name games, that the movement must be made *standing in place.* Otherwise, you take the risk of students falling in a heap on the floor or colliding in the center of the circle.

☺   *ACTIVITY: STICK GAME.* Using a yard stick, pointer (or any object that can be passed around), pantomime making it into something else, e.g., a toothbrush, guitar, canoe paddle, basketball, and have the class guess what it is. Establish a rhythm with clapping, and pass the stick or object back and forth to each member of the group. At first, take volunteers who have ideas of what the stick can become. Then, if a number of students are failing to use their imaginations, or to participate, start a

Variation: Stick Race. Set a time limit (which you can refer to as the "world record") of maybe three minutes (longer with primary grades). At a signal from you, one student will "do a stick" (change it into something). When someone guesses correctly what the stick is, the student can pass the stick on to the person to their right in the circle. That student has to pantomime something until someone guesses it. The object is to get the stick all the way around the circle and set a new record. Tell students if the stick gets to them and they can't think of anything new, just pantomime one of the objects they have already seen, so the game can keep going. This gives the shy students an "out" if they can't come up with a new idea spontaneously.

♪ *NOTE:* The stick game is an excellent way to stimulate the imagination and get the creative juices flowing.

♪ *NOTE:* Emphasize awareness of space when swinging the stick. Students should come to the center of the circle, away from the others, and if they have to swing the stick (as with baseball bats or swords), they should do it in slow motion so as not to hurt anyone.

☺ *ACTIVITIES: ADD-ONS.* (Also called "Parts of a Whole" games)

Statues: Create a group statue with the bodies of the entire class. Students volunteer to join in by raising their hands. The first person chosen enters the "stage," or center of the circle, takes a position and freezes. The second person who joins must connect to the first person, adding a piece to the statue which "fits" (again, no real right or wrong) with the "whole" that is already there. The third person adds another piece to the whole, etc., until all students are parts of the same abstract statue.

Machine: Build a machine by repeating the same format as above. This time, however, each person must come in with a repetitive sound and mechanical movement such as a machine part might have. After all the students have become parts of the machine, call out variations such as: an old rusty machine; a bright, new, shiny machine; a war machine; a silly machine; and finally a machine that gradually runs down and stops. Statues and Machines are very good for learning to work together as a team.

Pantomime Scene: The first person, by performing an activity in pantomime, establishes the location or environment of a scene, e.g., an office, a beach, a restaurant kitchen, etc. Each new person, in pantomime, adds a part to the environment--either a person, thing, animal, or anything they can imagine. Continue the pantomime until all students are participating.

Verbal Scene: Repeat the same format as with the Pantomime Scene above, but this time add words. Each person entering must establish who they are in relationship to someone who is in the scene already. The first person establishes the environment by either words or actions.

Scene Transformations: Same as above, except each person who comes into the scene must transform it into a totally new scene with new characters and new environment, by using actions and speech. Immediately, all actors already in the scene must change to a character in the new scene. This takes a little practice, but it is great fun, once mastered. The person entering must take focus in order to effectively change the scene.

♪ *NOTE*: Scene transformations help students to learn how to "take" a scene and how to respond quickly to new situations. Cooperation, paying attention, and following directions are also inherent in the mastering of this activity.

Variation: Curricular Themes. Stipulate that the machine, statue, environment, etc. must have something to do with a currently studied theme, story, etc. For example, do a pantomime scene and specify the place as an Native American Indian village, a desert, or ancient Babylonia.

☺ *ACTIVITY: IMPROVISATION.* Small groups start with a topic, theme, set of objects to be included, characters to be included, or other initial set of parameters from which to construct a scene. They are to plan their improvisation to include them all. And it can, at the teacher's option (or the students' option) be verbal or pantomime. Emphasize the need to focus, not on exact dialogue, but on the sequence of events. Emphasize the idea of a beginning, middle and end. "I'm the Lone Ranger and he's the outlaw and we're going to fight" is not enough for a scene. How does the scene start? What are the events which lead to a fight? How will the audience know it is over?

☺ *ADVANCED IMPROVISATIONS: FIRST LINE/LAST LINE.* Two or three actors are selected to go on stage. The audience gives them the first line of the scene they are to improvise, and the last line. The less connected the lines are, the more interesting the scene will be.

♪ *NOTE:* Emphasize that the most difficult part of this activity may be remembering the last line!

Variation: Objects Improv. The same format may be used with the audience mentioning three imaginary objects which the players must then incorporate into a scene. The actors should not plan what they will do, but rather jump right in and start. When all three objects have been mentioned in a logical progression of dialogue, the scene is over. Call "cut."

Variation: Occupations Improv. The players are given occupations by the audience and improvise a scene in which the characters reveal their occupations by using dialogue and action (they shouldn't say "Hi, I am a doctor," but find a way to give the audience a clue).

Variation: Memory Marathon: First line/last line, three objects, and occupations are given to actors by the audience before the scene starts. Mastering this level is challenging and fun and, when accomplished, fosters an experience of great self-esteem.

✓   *TIP:* Every improvisation should be begun by at least one of the players doing a physical action. This,too, will get the creative juices flowing and will stimulate facility in dialogue.

POINTS FOR EMPHASIS IN PLAYING CLASSROOM GAMES

Warming up the group is a key factor. If students are not ready to do a given activity, perhaps they need a simpler one as a warmup. This is particularly true of shy groups. Try a mass activity. Groups provide anonymity and help the shy individual to be involved without fear of being the object of attention. After Tennis Ball, or Group Non-Stop Talking, or the Hello Game, students may be more receptive to being placed in the limelight. If not, keep working group games until they feel confident.

Like any games, theater games can be enjoyed again and again. Players will get better with repetition. And each game should be as new and fresh each time as it was the first time. Players should be encouraged to approach each game with the same fresh wonder they had the first time they played it.

Once students can create improvised scenes, they can easily extend that skill to the presentation of a whole play (several improvised scenes together) or to the creation of a scripted piece. Games can then be used to sharpen dramatic skills, e.g., characterization, verbal agility, concentration.

Games will never work the same way with any group. Find the way which will work for you with your particular group. If you fail the first time, try, try again. You will very quickly get to the point where you invent your own games and variations to achieve a specific objective. Experiment with the rules and the structures until you find the way in which you can best control the game for the maximum learning experience in your classroom.

DEVELOPING YOUR OWN ARTS-IN-EDUCATION ACTIVITIES

Whenever you play a game, whenever you create and tell a story, draw a picture, make up a song, move, write, or speak related to a curriculum or behavioral objective, you are using the arts to communicate information: You are doing arts-in-education.

In general, there are two ways to create arts-in-education experiences:

1) Start with an objective. This is the usual method for everyday activity planning.

2) Start with a game. This is a way to add to your arts-in-education "bag of tricks."

If you start with an objective, you are seeking a way of communicating the information and using the arts to do so. General formats for theatrical experiences include narratives (stories), games, rituals, and systems.

NARRATIVES

Can you make up a *story* that everyone can act out which will illustrate your objective?

Example: Narrative. One day Carmen built herself a machine which could travel from one dimension to another. Deciding to try it out, she suddenly found herself transported to the Land of Weights. The King took her on a tour and introduced her to his subjects, all the different units of weight. Carmen was delighted to learn that each unit knew its relationship to every other. The King's subjects illustrated these relationships by acting them out for her, i.e., how many ounces there are in a pound, how many pounds in a ton, and so forth. They showed her some examples of things that might be weighed with a particular unit of measure, e.g., a bag of potatoes weighs five pounds. Carmen returned home confident in her new-found knowledge.

GAMES

Games are a refreshing alternative to pop quizzes on information.

☺   **ACTIVITY: *QUIZ SHOW*.** Re-enact a quiz show in which the questions are all about numbers recognition. For example, "This contestant will score 100 points if they can make their body into the number 6 in five seconds! Ready, set, go!"

Simulation games are also valuable.

☺   **ACTIVITY: *DISCRIMINATION*.** Have students perform some regular activity such as making murals, but the blue-eyed people can't talk to or work with the brown-eyed people. Vary the game by giving one group less time and fewer materials with which to complete the same task.

Simulation games elicit feelings and explore motivations. These should be discussed after the activity is over.

You can also start with a traditional game and vary it. What does "Hide and Seek" teach? How could it be varied slightly and get another objective?

☺   **ACTIVITY: *LETTER RECOGNITION*.** Give all players letters of the alphabet to pin to their clothes. Instead of calling each player's name when they are found, whoever is "it" must call the letter on each player they find.

RITUALS

Rituals are simply activities done with intense concentration and wherein each action is performed with importance and meaning. Rituals might be used at holidays, for instance.

☺   **ACTIVITY: *GIFT RITUAL*.** For Chanukah, Christmas, Boxing Day, or Kwansaa, have each student create a drawing or clay sculpture or other symbolic representation of a gift they would like to give to the class, to their family, or to the world. (Gifts may be symbolic: A child who wanted to give the class "cooperation" might make a picture of two hands shaking; "family prosperity" might be symbolized by the drawing of a large dollar bill; the painting of a dove could represent a gift of "peace" to the world.) Let each student, in turn, silently place their gift on a holiday table with everyone silently watching.

SYSTEMS

A *system* is a related sequence of activities which together form a whole. Most complete educational activities are systems.

Example: System. Start by telling the story of Carmen, described under "Narratives;" then do a warm-up game of the machine (see *Machine*, p.37); then act out the story; draw a scene from it, illustrating the relationship of certain units of weight. End with a *Word Poem* (see below) based on all the students' drawings. Congratulations! You have a creative educational system.

THE WORD POEM

A poem is "an arrangement of words written or spoken... expressing experience, ideas, or emotions in a style more concentrated, imaginative, or powerful than that of ordinary speech or prose..."

A "word poem" has been described as "the collective celebration of an event." It is inevitably a very effective closing to any classroom experience.

After the event (story, performance, lesson), get *one* word from each participant which crystallizes the experience for them ("reminds you of what happened"). Write the words on a piece of paper or on the board, and tie them together in a meaningful way with your own connecting words.

From a class on Mexican culture, for instance, you might get such words as: siesta, charro, pesos, serape, sombrero, mestitzo, señorita, pueblo, hacienda and fiesta.

Obviously the words may be put together in many different ways. Here is one example, emphasizing new vocabulary:

> After his *siesta,*
> The *charro* took his last ten *pesos*
> To buy a new *serape.*
> Then, doffing his *sombrero*
> To the *mestitzo señorita,*
> He escorted her out of the *pueblo*
> To the big *hacienda*
> Where they sang and danced at the *fiesta.*

ACTIVITIES IN AWARENESS

Exercises in sense awareness are not only fun, revealing, and mind-expanding, they also have positive effects in the areas of behavior, notably trust, sensitivity, awareness, and cooperation.

☺ *ACTIVITY: LISTENING.* Have the class sit for one full minute with eyes closed in total silence, trying not to initiate any sound. First, they are to listen for any sounds they hear in the room or outside the room. Next, without shutting out sounds outside themselves, they are to listen, as well, for any sounds inside their own bodies. Again, without blocking out or holding on to any particular sounds, have them listen for a "center of silence" within their own hearts. Let them experience this for another minute or so. Then make them aware once again of sounds inside their bodies, then sounds outside their bodies, and gradually have them open their eyes and discuss their experiences.

☺ *ACTIVITY: HEARING RECALL.* Have students sit with their eyes closed and see if they can recreate in their minds the sounds of images you will give them, e.g., a railroad train, a freeway, a crowded street, walking on a leafy sidewalk, wind in the evergreens, a playground, and other strong, sound images. Discuss their experiences.

Variation: Other Senses. Repeat the Hearing Recall activity, substituting each of the other four senses, one at a time. For example, have them recall the *taste* of steak, spinach, ice cream, etc.; the *smell* of roses, garbage, perfume, etc.; the *feeling* of a pillow, rain on their faces, sun on the back of their neck, etc.; and the *sight* of a rainbow, a Christmas tree, a waterfall, etc.

♪ *NOTE:* Some images will invoke a variety of sense memories. The recalled sight of a Christmas tree, for instance, may stimulate the smell of pine needles, the sound of caroling, and the taste of hot chocolate. Lead students in a discussion of the relationship between the senses.

☺ *ACTIVITY: CONSCIOUSNESS WALK.* Have one student at a time stand on one side of your room. Have each of them focus their attention about six feet ahead.
A path should be cleared through the room to allow the students to pass freely from one side to the other.
Each student should now begin to walk slowly and easily through the room toward the other side in complete silence.
Tell students to allow the conscious mind to receive all of the room, much like a motion picture, rather than a series of snapshots. They should be aware of the changes in patterns, colors, sizes, shadows, and all sorts of objects. Students should not turn their heads from side to side, but focus straight in front, using peripheral vision to take in the room. They should focus in space, rather than on any specific thing. If possible, they should not blink.
Tell them to allow their minds to focus and, as physical movements become slower and more sustained, to allow their focused minds to settle into a dreamlike state until their total self is "in sync" and their body is gliding through space.

When they reach the other side, the students should dwell in silence on what they have seen and felt.

With any exercise in awareness, always refrain from talking before the experience has been thoroughly assimilated by the conscious mind. The objective of these activities is to focus on the senses, rather than the intellectualization of the experience.

Do these activities yourself, at home or in your room, before trying them with students, until you recognize the feelings they generate. The feelings are good and you will want to share them.

"Make the most of every sense; glory in all facets of pleasure and beauty that the world reveals to you."

Helen Keller

CHAPTER THREE

THEATER ARTS
AS TEACHING STRATEGIES

"Where the arts have demanded and achieved equal recognition with other disciplines, marked improvement in learning skills has resulted."

"The Arts in Education and Basic Skills"
Kathryn Bloom, The JDR Fund, 1976

MAKING CONNECTIONS

The secret to using the arts effectively as teaching strategies is in learning to make connections, in seeing everything as a whole unto itself.

This is not always as easy as it sounds. As mentioned elsewhere in this book, most of us have not been brought up to think this way. Rather we tend to grow up with a somewhat fragmented view of life. There's one's job and one's home life, one's dreams and the "reality" of life. There's school and the "real world," the arts and "practical" matters. Even Life and Death are looked upon as two separate and distinct conditions, rather than being aspects of a continuous process. Separation of ideas, feelings, and activities are a way of life to most of us, and often we are adamant about "drawing the line."

Artists, however, seldom think in such pigeon-holed patterns. When they read the poet William Blake's oft-quoted observation of "the universe in a grain of sand," they tend to identify with the image immediately. "And not only a grain of sand," they may think, "but everything!"

Each part contains within it the whole, just as the seed contains the tree, or the DNA pattern contains the individual, just as a complete organism might be replicated from a single cell.

Each entity is a symbol for all other entities, from an artist's point of view. The universe exists not only in a grain of sand, but as well in the song of a bird, the laughter of a child, or the interaction of the wind and the trees.

From such thinking, the principle of holography developed (for artists and scientists think surprisingly alike... someone has said science and magic are merely two ways of looking at the same phenomenon). In holography, a three-dimensional representation of an object is projected from many photo-images, each containing the image of the whole object and each projected from different angles.

This principle has led many physicists to speculate on a "holographic universe" - each electron which makes up our perceivable reality containing within it the essence of all of it.

Extrapolation is the key word.

"The arts, when well taught, provide children with opportunities to use their imagination, to create multiple solutions to problems, and to rely on their own judgment to determine when a problem is solved or a project is completed. In the arts, there is no rule to 'prove' the correctness of an answer and no formula to determine when a task is complete. In the arts, children must rely on that most exquisite of human intellectual abilities--judgment."

Elliot W. Eisner
Stanford University

☺ *ACTIVITY: STRETCHING THE IMAGE WITH WORDS*. Take a word--just about any word--and *stretch the image* as far as it will go. Do more than stretch it... expand it to the outer limits of your imagination!

Take the word "bird," for example. Free associate. Start with ideas like wing, feathers, flight, air, sky, swoop, soar, glide, etc. Then go further and expand it into the realm of symbols: grace, freedom, speed, far-seeing, overview, ecstasy. Stretch again: omen, messenger, holiness, spirit, soul, peace, happiness, etc. See how far you've come just with a simple word?

Or try the word "fire": heat, flame, consume, volcano, campfire, torch, candle, inferno, holocaust. Light, purification, destruction, home, civilization, energy. Armies, Prometheus, sacred, life, the sun, spirit, etc.

Have your students come up with their own words. It's a fun activity for the mind and it certainly leads you to an out-of-the-ordinary view of the world around you.

Now try extrapolating images into activities for your students. *Look for relationships*. Don't be awed by the possibilities or what you might have thought were the limits of your imagination. If you can extrapolate "bird" into "soul" and "fire" into "life," you can transcend any limits you choose. Here are some examples of stretching the image in the curriculum:

☺ *ACTIVITY: CREATIVE CURRICULUM EXTRAPOLATION*. Pick a curriculum objective; for instance, an introduction to the life of the Native American Indians. How can you convey the information your students need to learn through visual art? Pictures in textbooks and posters are helpful; so is having the children draw pictures of Native Americans.

Stretch the image further. Extrapolate. What about taking them on a field trip in the woods, of having them bring natural objects from home: feathers, shells, dried weeds, colorful stones? Then have them create jewelry or articles of clothing for themselves, just like the Native Americans did.

Or bring an old sheet from home and build a small tipi in one corner of your room. Let each child choose an Indian name from nature (a combination of an adjective and noun usually work, such as "running deer," "bright feather," or "whispering wind"). Stretch the image by naming themselves in contemporary terms, e.g., "Nose in Book," "TV Watcher," etc. Have them create a visual symbol for that name and paint it on the tipi. Instead of merely letting them listen to recordings of Indian music (although a fine activity to inspire them), let them create their own music from beating on sticks, on bottoms of upside-down wastebaskets, or from clacking together stones. Guide them into finding different rhythms and even communicating with sound alone.

Or have each child bring a blanket from home and sit them in a circle wrapped in their blankets and, through discussion, let the group decide something of relevance to the whole class. Encourage them to refer to each other as "brother" and "sister." Turn off the electricity in the room so that they have only natural light to see by. Better still, hold a class outdoors.

Instead of just telling them how the buffalo was so important to the Native Americans, divide the class into groups and have one group act out a buffalo hunt and other groups act out using the buffalo for clothing, shelter, food, weapons, tools, and art.

If you want your students to *learn* about Native Americans, let them *be* Native Americans for a little while.

☺ ***ACTIVITY: INTEGRATING MATH WITH THE AMERICAN REVOLUTION***. In math, develop an imaginary budget for financing the American Revolution and help your students to figure out how much it cost to feed, clothe, and outfit an army. Let them act out a budget committee; or George Washington receiving a government allotment and, with his officers, figuring out how to spend it.

☺ ***ACTIVITY: SCIENCE EXTRAPOLATION***. For a science objective, let students act out an expedition from another planet and explore the rocks, plants, animals, and even the atmosphere of the planet Earth. Have them identify certain environmental conditions similar to those on their "home planet" and propose possible solutions.

☺ ***ACTIVITY: MOUNT OLYMPUS GAME***. Let them pretend to be Greek gods and goddesses looking down on Earth and discussing what they see: pollution and the environment, the international situation, the community in which they live, even their daily lives at school and in their particular classroom. If each student is assigned a particular god or goddess, then with even a minimum amount of research on their parts, they can look at issues and events from differing points of view. This can lead to fruitful discussions.

☺ ***ACTIVITY: MAGIC AND SCIENCE***. In language arts, let them explain a scientific phenomenon as magicians, e.g., "The very essence of each and every thing is a teeny-weeny castle. This castle is called Nucleus Hall. Inside the castle, live tiny, little spirits, a whole family of them: the Proton family. All the little Protons and their cousin Neutrons are very sad and just mope around, never going outside their castle. Meanwhile, the royal guard, the Mighty Electrons, march round and round protecting the Proton Family and the castle from invaders." Then have them describe a magical happening as scientists, e.g., "The appearance of the prince being transformed into a frog may be explained as a rearrangement of the atomic structure of the cells in his body to more closely approximate the atomic structure of the cells of an amphibian." Students may draw pictures of the phenomena explained, write poems or stories about them, or act them out.
For further extrapolation, lead students into the exploration of various atomic and/or molecular structures or, in the case of the frog prince, the changes in molecular DNA structure which cause mutations.

☺ ***ACTIVITY: STONE SOUP CELEBRATION***. Have your students invite their parents to help them actually prepare "stone soup" as they act out the story "Stone Soup." Let them set up a "village" in the classroom by making floor-to-ceiling panels of butcher paper painted to look like houses. Help them to make tricorn hats and bandoliers for the boys, babushkas and aprons for the girls. Teach them a song and dance the villagers can perform at the end of the story. Give each student an occupation, a name, and a position in the community (see *Characterization*, p.83).

Let the study of the story be a celebrative experience. Change their perspective again and again. Explore different points of view. Encourage them to think creatively. Challenge them to be original.

Refer to *"The Elements of Creativity"* below and *"Symbols"* (p.52). Make every new unit an adventure. You'll find their understanding, retention, and excitement increase as you engage their senses, their feelings, and their bodies. And you'll be reminded why you chose to be a teacher out of all the professions in the world.

THE ELEMENTS OF CREATIVITY

We *all* create! We can't help but create! We're creating all the time! That's what humans do. We create! We create the world we live in with every breath. We create our lives with every action we take, with every word we speak. We create things like automobiles and traffic patterns, loaves of bread and meals, money and economic systems, building and homes, offices and temples. We create belief systems and principles, laws, and taxes and then we arrange our lives to conform to our creations.

We create children and contracts, love letters and debts, bank accounts and lifestyles. The legacy we leave the world at the end of our days is that which we have created.

How do we do this? Through our thoughts, feelings, and actions. Our thoughts are limited only by our willingness to think. Our feelings are tempered only by the ideals and principles we have created by our thoughts. Thoughts can control feelings. What, then, can control thoughts? Will, perhaps? Can we choose what we think? Of course we can. We consistently do--all the time. How else could we accomplish even the simplest act of putting on our clothes, or getting from one place to another?

The elements we use in creation are space, time, light, color, line, shape, form, movement, sound, pattern, and texture.

☺   *ACTIVITY: OBSERVATION*. To increase your students' awareness of any individual element of creativity, have them sit in a circle and give round robin observations. They are to pay attention to the element being focused on, and speak about what they notice. For instance, with **light**, you might find students say: "I notice it is darkest in this corner," or "I notice the light coming through the window." Keep them speaking in the first person and in the present tense in order to focus their attention on their experience of the moment.

After all the obvious observations about light are made, they will start to stretch their imaginations more, the longer you play, e.g., "I notice that because of the peaks and valleys in the carpet, the light (and the shadows it creates) makes a wide variety of shades and colors."

Creation begins with filling **space**: A blank piece of paper, an empty canvas, a bare stage, an open expanse of land. Then, **time**: a dividing up of what is, what was, and what will be. Time and space are the parents of our existence.

Art begins with **light**, the concentrated, radiant energy which ultimately enables us to exist in time. Light is the essence of creative action, whether it be the invisible light in our minds, or the visible light we receive through our external sense of sight. Light allows us to discriminate one thing from another.

Because light radiates (that is, moves from one place to another), **movement** becomes a second component of art and a fourth element of creativity: movement in space over time.

As light radiates, it is refracted into **color**, as in a rainbow. (And speaking of rainbows, there are seven colors in a rainbow, not five or six as usually depicted in popular graphics and illustrations. Try inserting indigo, or blue-violet, between the blue and violet rays of a rainbow and watch it become magical!)

As light moves through space over time from one point to another point, it traces a **line** which, in turn, is the primary element of **shape**. Shape is the result of intersecting lines in the same plane.

Thus far, we have covered only two dimensions. A line creates the first dimension, and the intersection of two lines adds a second, a flat plane.

With a third dimension, we can create **form**, the substantial multiplication of shapes (a cube derived from squares, a pyramid from triangles, a sphere from circles, etc.).

Sound, being vibration, accompanies movement and, scientifically, all movement is recognized as producing sound. Even in two-dimensional art, such as drawing or painting, we speak of lyricism or dynamics--attributes of sound.

With **pattern**, or design, we move into the arrangement of the components thus far noted and introduce the individuality of the artist. The uniqueness of any work of art is identified through its pattern or design.

Pattern, applied to time, creates **rhythm**.

Finally, **texture** enables the recipient of the creative act to respond specifically to the work through direct, sensory involvement.

To attempt to establish a standard linear arrangement of aesthetic elements would merely be an arguable academic activity. Regardless of the perspective of the thinker, the components of the creative process are Space, Time, Light, Color, Movement, Sound, Line, Shape, Form, Pattern, and Texture. These are the building blocks of our universe--whether the one we live in or the one we create.

"Art is a system invented by nature to enable human beings to come into full possession of their higher senses. It is a form of wealth in which all can share and which is dependent not on ownership but on desire and perception."

Norman Cousins

CREATION

First there was an explosion somewhere in space,
A big bang in the midst of the stars.
What caused it?
Who knows?
Whatever makes things go bang, I suppose.
And out of that flash came a rain of sparks,
Millions upon billions, trillions, quadrillions,
Duodecillions!
And more!
Always more.
All ways more!
And God said, "Let there be light!"
And there was Light!

Those sparks, when they met, formed little atoms
And the atoms formed gases
And the gases formed liquids.
Then the brightest of the sparks, which we call our Sun,
Blazed forth his great warmth!
Then came cooling winds and the liquids became solid
And a planet was formed
And this place we call "here" began.
As the liquids cooled, they became river and rock,
Ocean and continent, mountain and plain,
And the earth formed its body.
And it moved and squirmed and vomited and belched,
Like all newborns will;
And as it turned and shifted, new mountains were born
And they spewed forth their insides,
Which hardened in time, became new land and changed landscapes.
And some of those sparks changed shape and became plants,
Great cedars and pine trees, delicate flowers and moss.
The great Sun shone upon them and they gave forth their perfume,
Which he warmed with his breath and turned into rain.
And the plant kingdom gave birth to forests and grasses.
The earth expressed Life!

From "Aspen Hill Anthology"
CES

THE CREATIVE CLASSROOM

A creative classroom is one in which the individual creative spirit of every student is educated ("drawn forth"). It is a place where dissemination of information is no more important than the continuing development of skills to *use* that information practically and productively. For a classroom to be truly creative, it must provide an environment which honors the elements of creativity, nurtures the creative process, and celebrates the creative act.

The education of one's senses and one's feelings must be given equal attention to the education of one's mind in the creative classroom.

Most kindergartens are creative classrooms, as are many first, second, and sometimes third grades; that is, they are bright, attractive, interesting rooms to be in. Lots of learning games are played, kinesthetic activities are encouraged; art, music, and creative drama are seen as a normal part of the school curriculum. School is an interesting and exciting place to most primary students. ☺

It is in the intermediate and junior high grades that many students--far too many students-begin to lose interest in learning.

Why?

At the age of about nine or ten, a child's social opportunities broaden. Peer pressure to follow certain mores and fads becomes stronger as children approach adolescence. Curriculum studies develop increasing demands for acquiring and storing facts as children progress through higher levels of learning. And, all too often, by the time a child has reached the seventh or eighth grade, the love of learning which burned so brightly during the first few years of school has diminished--somehow transformed into attitudes of duty, responsibility, even resentment. The world outside has become a symbol of freedom and opportunity, and the classroom a necessary obligation. Some children even come to "hate" school. Learning, for them, has become joyless, an onerous task which they have no choice but to perform according to the law of the land.

Unfortunately, this condition is evidenced by the vast numbers of children who drop out of junior highs and high schools all over the country--hundreds of thousands of them every year! Illiteracy, both linguistic and cultural, has become a national problem and a national disgrace. American schools rank embarrassingly low in world surveys on educational quality. And excellence in education is so far from being a standard as to be newsworthy when it emerges.

Establishing and maintaining every classroom as a haven for creativity may not answer all the problems which beset our schools. But it can give each child the opportunity to develop their creative potential throughout the formative years. It can compete with the "world outside" by offering an excitement and a fresh wonder equivalent to a shopping mall, most TV programming for young people, and pop music.

Virtually every educator who has recently come into national prominence for excellence in teaching has demonstrated principles inherent in a creative classroom. In a great number of cases, they integrated the arts into their curriculum and inspired their students by getting them to *participate* in their own learning.

In every case, they have utilized the elements of creativity in their teaching. So can you.

"Communication is a combination of psychology and theater."
WTS

SYMBOLS

We live in a sea of symbols. We move through feeling-worlds of meaning. Consider the dove, the eagle, the vulture; the cross, the star, the swastika, the crown and scepter, the dollar sign, the face, the hand, the eye... ♥ With each of these words, be aware of the multitude of images, feelings, and thoughts which well up inside you.

Reality exists within our beingness as well as in the outer world of perceptions. How we *feel* about a thing is equal in importance to how we *think* about it. *And the only difference between us and our children in this respect is that they don't have as extensive a vocabulary to express how they feel and think.*

A *symbol* is the representation of these thoughts and feelings. Words are symbols. So also are numbers, shapes, colors, objects, and designs. ☺

Since this is a book on the application of the arts to education, let's focus our immediate attention on the traditional symbolic interpretation of the components of the creative/artistic process.

Space: The word-concept of "space" symbolizes such things as: possibility, freedom, adventure, mystery, openness, creativity itself.

Time: Order, separation, structure, restriction, cycles, the creative process.

Light: Realization, happiness, knowledge, life, radiance.

Color: Different colors symbolize a wide variety of different things. (See *Color*, p.55)

Movement: Shape, duration, acceleration, intensity, rhythm, direction and quality of movement can powerfully suggest both mood and meaning in any art form, thus symbolizing various kinds of human behavior.

Sound: Sound is a most powerful mood-motivator. Some researchers maintain, for example, that different kinds of music actually stimulate parts of our bodies; rock and roll--our genital area; marches--our stomachs; romantic music--our hearts; and classical music--our brains. Try it and see what you think--*and feel.*

Line: (see *Line*, p.58)

Shape: Shapes (the circle, the crescent, the triangle, and the square, for example) have different symbolic meanings in religions, national cultures, philosophical systems, and to the public at large.

Form: Forms are three-dimensional shapes and, as such, have even more potent symbolic meanings: the pyramid, the sphere, and the cube, for instance. The globe, synonymous with the sphere, has even become a symbol for our planet.

Pattern: Pattern gives any shape or form distinction or individuality. The same shape or form patterned with plaids, polka dots, stripes, or paisley conveys extremely different qualities, thus changing the specific symbolism of the shape or form itself. The varieties of decorated Easter eggs are excellent examples of this principle.

Texture: Texture relates strongly to our tactile sense. Smooth, rough, slick, soft, hard, spongy, jagged, sharp, etc., conjure up meaningful symbolic images in all aspects of our sensory experience.

☺ *ACTIVITY: COLOR WORD POEM.* Choose image words stimulated by different colors; write them on the board and use them to create a poem which expresses feelings. For example, for "red" you might get "passion," "angry," "blood," "war," "energy," "action," etc. Make these into a poem (see *Word Poem*, p.41).

☺ *ACTIVITY: COLOR COMBINATION POEM.* Find words and phrases which express your associations with combinations of color. Use them to write a poem about your feelings for a holiday. For example, after finding words and phrases to associate with orange and with black, write a poem about Halloween.

☺ *ACTIVITY: COLOR COMBINATION FEELINGS.* Discuss how you feel when you put different combinations of colors together. For example, how would you feel if the classroom were painted sky blue and violet? Orange and yellow?

☺ *ACTIVITY: COLOR COMBINATION PATTERNS.* Try designing the same Valentine patterns (or Christmas trees, American flags, or jack-o-lanterns) using different colors, e.g., yellow hearts, green lace and red doves, or gold hearts, purple lace and blue doves, or any other combination of colors. Choose the one you like best and tell why.

☺ *ACTIVITY: MOVEMENT QUALITIES.* Have students move in circles, squares, triangles, etc. (see *Line*, p.58). Pick two points on opposite sides of the room (space) and have students move from one to another in various manners: fast then slow, forcefully then gently, to different rhythms, back and forth, facing forwards and backwards, and with different qualities, e.g., mysteriously, lackadaisically, carefully, quietly, brashly.
Then ask them to write or discuss how they felt and what they perceived.

☺ *ACTIVITY: LISTENING.* (see p.42)

☺ *ACTIVITY: SHAPE MEANINGS.* Draw on the board the following symbols: a circle, a square, a triangle, a five-pointed star, a six-pointed star, the combination of a star and a crescent, stars and stripes, etc. Ask students to write down meanings they attach to each. Compare.

☺ *ACTIVITY: SHAPES IN CULTURE.* For a particular culture, geographical region, historical period, or other social studies thematic unit, assign some students to research the symbols associated with that period (government, culture, etc). Have them create the symbols from construction paper, remaining as true to the original as possible. Post the symbols in your room and allow students to comment, after living with them for awhile, on how they feel about them.

☺ *ACTIVITY: FORMS IN CULTURE.* Have students repeat the activity immediately above (on shapes in culture) with three dimensional forms.

☺ ☺ ☺   *ACTIVITY: PATTERNMAKING.* There are many techniques for making patterns: block-prints carved out of linoleum or wood; block prints carved out of half a raw potato; stencils made out of pieces of cardboard or other suitable material; or sponges, cut in the desired shape. Have your class create either patterned environments or patterned clothes.

To do environments, cut three lengths of butcher paper for each environment you wish to create (perhaps one for each corner of the room). Arrange the sheets to hang ceiling to floor. Before hanging permanently, have students take their pattern maker (sponge, potato, stencil or whatever) and pattern the butcher paper. For example, one group might choose a brick pattern, very easy to accomplish with a square sponge dipped in watered down red paint and applied in the typical alternating pattern of a brick wall; another group might choose a pattern of polka dots made with a potato dipped in red paint and applied randomly to their sheets of butcher paper. Hang the sheets of the same pattern together in a corner and explore how it feels to sit in each environment. Describe the feelings. (This is a great way to construct simple suggestive sets for a classroom play project, by the way; e.g., create simple homes of bricks for "Stone Soup" and cut out simple squares of a different colored paper to paste on for windows or doors.)

For clothes, have students bring in some plain piece of clothing they can paint (old T-shirts are ideal). Have them create pattern makers from sponges, potatoes, or stencils, and apply them to the clothes. Have them model the clothes in front of mirrors and describe their impressions and feelings about each pattern.

☺   *ACTIVITY: PATTERNS IN PRIMARY COLORS.* With red, yellow, and blue markers (crayons or paints will do just as nicely) have each student create a color pattern which repeats itself on a piece of paper. Compare the different patterns each has created. Note the variety of patterns which can be created with just three colors. See which patterns create a distinct feeling or image for anyone else.

☺   *ACTIVITY: TEXTURE EXPLORATION.* Bring in several strongly textured items, e.g., a piece of velvet, a piece of burlap, a piece of silk, an orange peel, plastic, glass, an open pine cone. Place them each in a separate paper bag. Pass the bags around the class. Have students place their hands into each bag without looking and experience each texture. Ask them to choose one bag and write about images associated with the texture inside. Alternatively, they may draw images, or act them out in groups.

Aesthetic literacy demands that we be aware sensorially of what's going on around us and how it affects what's going on inside us. Why should psychologists, visual artists, and Madison Avenue have all the fun?

Helping students to focus upon and become aware of these creative elements will help them to sharpen their aesthetic perceptions and give them a richer experience of the world around them.

COLOR

In different cultures, different colors may take on different meanings. For example, in China, white is the color associated with death, whereas in the Western world, death is represented by black; in Elizabethan England, blue was the color of servitude; and in contemporary society, pink is more often seen as a feminine rather than a masculine color. Again, the *reasons* for our responses to colors are buried deep within our individual and collective psyches. It is undeniable, however, that color produces potent emotional and intellectual reactions in us.

Studies have demonstrated that violent criminals become docile in a pink room. Red excites us. Most schoolrooms and hospital rooms used to be painted a pale green. Our language gives evidence to our symbolic interpretations of color. Expressions like "in the pink," "green with envy," "feeling blue," "in a black mood," "seeing red," etc., actually use colors to express precise feelings.

It is said, nowadays, that infants are most attracted to black and white. That makes sense. Black (the synthesis of pigmented color) and white (the synthesis of colored light) contain all the essential elements of visual differentiation. For a new mind to assimilate and order its experience, it must be able to first distinguish one object from another. Black and white serve as standards of distinction.

As the young mind continues to expand, it may discriminate more subtly through the gradations of color. The very small child will inevitably be attracted to bright colors. Only as children begin to develop some social awareness will they be likely to become attuned to shades, hues, and tones. As maturity develops, certain colors will become their "favorites," according to their largely unconscious associations of particular colors with significant intellectual and emotional experiences, both culturally and personally.

These are the traditional Western interpretations of basic colors:

White: Though technically not a color, it possesses the attributes of a color and conveys purity, innocence, upliftment of mind, spirit, and light. The wedding dress is traditionally white in our culture. Until recently, the white shirt (or "white collar") indicated a whole lifestyle of respectability and sincerity. The cowboy with the white hat is the proverbial "good guy." Added to any other color, white softens and lightens the color. This is true psychologically as well as physically.

Red: The color of action, danger, passion, sex, the vibrancy of life. Pink, a mixture of red (passion) and white (purity), is generally interpreted as affection. Pink is a youthful color, somewhat frivolous, more for play than for work. Hot pink is bolder, more blatant and closer to red.

Orange: Personality, self-expression, and bravado is communicated by orange, a combination of red (passion or action) and yellow (mental activity). Orange attracts attention. It says, "Look at me! Here I am!" Life jackets are usually orange, as are hunters' caps and jackets and the garb of highway workers.

Yellow: Brightness, the sun, intelligence, cowardice (an excess of mental activity?), and life. Yellow is usually a life-celebrating color, often used for joyous occasions.

Green: Healing and growth are the symbolic properties of green - the life of Nature, money as a medium of exchange, fertility. The Girl Scouts of America think of green as the color of love.

Blue: Truth ("true blue"), loyalty, water, space, emotion, honesty. In its most radiant hue, it is called "royal." Baby blue is ascribed to boys in the Western world. Blue ranks as the all-time favorite color for most people. Blue forget-me-nots are the romantic symbol of fidelity. And "blue Monday" and "the blues" notwithstanding, it is the bluebird which we associate with the quality of happiness.

Indigo: According to Webster, indigo is "a deep violet-blue, designated by Newton as one of the seven prismatic or primary colors." Indigo may be interpreted as Mystery, the night sky or magic.

Purple: Blue ("truth") and red ("action") combine to suggest purple ("service"). Purple (closely associated with violet, which is actually bluer than purple, yet less blue than indigo) is the color of royalty and of sacrifice. For centuries, purple was exclusively the color of kings and was highly valued (partly because the dye was expensively extracted from shellfish in a limited geographic area in the Middle East). Bold and direct, purple suggests a strong identity.

Black: This synthesis of pigmented color is interpreted in the West as the color of death, mourning, deepest mystery, sophistication and formality. Black added to any color intensifies that color's symbolic meaning.

Brown: Blended by combining red ("action") and green ("life"), brown is the color of the earth and connotes solidity, simplicity, comfortable familiarity and a sense of rustic construction. Brown conveys images of Franciscan monks and Teddy bears.

Metallic Colors (gold, silver, copper): These suggest a higher octave of interpretation and may be designated as "spiritualized" colors. Gold suggests spiritualized intelligence or the highest order of mental activity, thus the gold crown on the head of a monarch, or the phrases "golden opportunity" and "golden age." Silver (spiritualized white) is strongly associated with elegance, distinguished accomplishment, or the respected medium of monetary exchange. And copper (or bronze), being the color of the earth raised to a new level of vibration, can be interpreted as symbolic of man's utilization of the minerals of the earth.

Be Still and reflect -
not on the mechanics of change,
but on the miracle of change.
As you read,
allow in your mind
the image of a prism
to form.
Now, on one side,
see a pure, white shaft
of light
entering the prism.
Now, on the other side,
see a rainbow of colors
flowing,
out.
Actually see clear light
entering on the one side
and a rainbow
flowing from the other...
Feel the moment of change,
experience the change
Become the Change...

Allow your thoughts to drift away,
allow your mind to be still.
Feel, experience, live now
be still,
be here
now,
I Am
experience.
I Am
the light,
the prism
and the rainbow
and what I see with my mind,
I feel with my total being
and
I am One with it.

WTS

LINE

An important principle in blocking stage movement and choreography in dance, line may also be symbolically relevant in visual art.

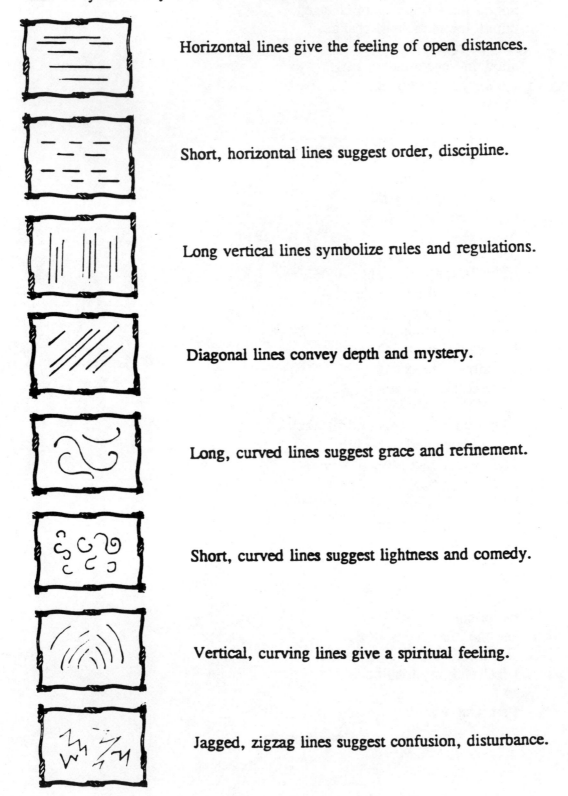

Horizontal lines give the feeling of open distances.

Short, horizontal lines suggest order, discipline.

Long vertical lines symbolize rules and regulations.

Diagonal lines convey depth and mystery.

Long, curved lines suggest grace and refinement.

Short, curved lines suggest lightness and comedy.

Vertical, curving lines give a spiritual feeling.

Jagged, zigzag lines suggest confusion, disturbance.

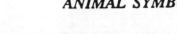

ANIMAL SYMBOLS

Dove:	Peace
Eagle:	Strength, power, mobility
Raven:	Mystery
Turkey:	Foolishness, ineptitude
Lion:	Courage, nobility
Fox:	Cunning
Dog:	Humility, playfulness, friendship
Cat:	Superiority, aloofness
Pig:	Stupidity, gluttony
Serpent:	Wisdom, danger, death
Monkey:	Silliness, carelessness
Chicken:	Cowardice
Goose:	Silliness
Beaver:	Industry, busy-ness
Elephant:	Strength, memory
Mule:	Stubbornness
Peacock:	Pride
Rabbit:	Timidity, quickness
Dragon:	Harmony, good fortune
Coyote:	Cleverness
Opossum:	Trickiness

ACTIVITY: ANIMAL CHARACTERIZATION.

a. Have your students act out each of the above animals in pantomime, expressing their symbolic qualities, as listed above.

b. Then have them first write and then speak a simple sentence which expresses what the animal might say about itself and *how* it might sound. For example, Lion: (speaking loudly, in a confident tone) "I'm king of the beasts and lord of the jungle. No one is braver than I."

c. Next have them pantomime a human with these symbolic animal characteristics. For instance, a samurai warrior might adopt the attitude of a lion; so might a knight (such as Richard the Lion-Hearted).

d. Finally, have them write and/or speak lines as human characters with animal qualities, while walking appropriately, e.g., (striding powerfully to the crest of the hill), "I challenge any knight to joust with me. Let him who thinks he's a better man step forward and confront me squarely."

This is an excellent introduction to characterization when acting out any story or play.

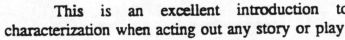
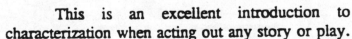

CHAPTER FOUR

DESIGNING THE ARTS-BASED THEMATIC CURRICULUM

This chapter deals with the subject of how to teach your entire curriculum through the arts.

Webster defines the word "course" as "an onward movement; a going on from one point to the next; progress." Life is like that. And so is a curriculum of studies--which the dictionary tells us is a series of required courses. As one's life must be balanced in order to be fulfilled, so must a curriculum.

A balanced life is neither fragmented nor compartmentalized into categories of activities. There are few of us who can enjoy a social life without family and profession influencing our enjoyment. Inevitably, our intellectual pursuits, our friendships, our amusements, even our goals and aspirations are colored by our economic status, our parental responsibility, our state of health, the political context in which we live, and the infinite details which make up our individual lives.

Traditionally, curricula in American schools have been divided at every grade level into separate studies of subject matter: language arts, history-social studies, mathematics, science, physical education, and the visual and performing arts. All too often, these disciplines have been taught with such an exclusivity they have seemed totally unrelated to each other.

Students educated within such artificial boundaries will often attempt to apply similar restrictions to the various aspects of their lives. Their point of view and resultant behavior sometimes alter radically, depending on whether they are at school, at home, with family, with friends, or alone. And when they graduate and discover the world is a whole greater than the sum of its parts, many cannot adapt. They have had no training in relating to wholeness.

In recognition of this potentially undesirable outcome of thirteen years of public schooling, educators continually strive to develop strategies which will integrate curriculum studies. These simulate the integrated quality of life in the "real world." One of these strategies which has surfaced from time to time during the developing history of American education is the thematic curriculum.

Whereas our lives are not, in reality, sharply divided into separate and distinct functions, we experience certain episodes in our lives which seem to revolve around particular themes. Entering school, puberty, adolescence, higher education, career, military service, marriage, and parenthood are common examples. Thus the concept of developing a curriculum around themes which communicate significant educational objectives seems to be a natural process. This is often quite effective in helping students to integrate their studies with their lives. Undoubtedly, this is why the thematic curriculum is enjoying a renewed popularity among teachers charged with leading youngsters into the 21st century, in such a way that the students are prepared to cope with an unimaginably complex society.

The visual and performing arts provide an ideal tool for integrating the disparate elements of a curriculum into a thematic unit. The arts (and the language arts must also be considered within this classification) appeal to the senses and emotions as well as the intellect. They form a bridge between different aspects of any cultural phenomenon and may be used to blend distinct pieces of information into a comprehensible whole.

Supplemented with contemporary newspaper accounts and photographs, diary entries, military maps, recordings of contemporary music, student improvisations of key events, and biographical accounts of political and military leaders, it is quite likely such an arts-based thematic curriculum unit will be significantly more effective in communicating an understanding of any historical period than the traditional lecture and textbook reading assignment approach which prevails in most schools. Certainly, to most of today's media-drenched students, it would be more interesting. *Drums Along the Mohawk, The Last Emperor, The Prince and the Pauper, The Rise and Fall of the Third Reich, Clan of the Cave Bear, Messenger of God, The Best Years of our Lives, Grapes of Wrath, Citizen Kane, Glory, Dances With Wolves, The Last of the Mohicans, The Black Robe* and just about any of Shakespeare's plays are examples, among countless films, plays and/or novels, which hold vast treasures of educational material put into perspective for history and social science objectives.

Scientific principles such as the nature of cycles, or electricity, or the theory of evolution may be explored through literary works; improvisational simulations; paintings and sculpture; classical, popular, and folk music; book illustrations, architecture, and miniature models; dance and pantomime representing symbolic movement patterns; costumes, scenery, stage properties; and even more "avant garde" forms, such as performance art (which is a form describing some of the more impressive exhibits at today's science fairs).

Mathematical concepts may be integrated into virtually any thematic curriculum by virtue of the symbolic and functional use of numbers in any depiction of human or natural activity. Money, for instance, has been used as a medium of exchange in almost every culture. Geometry has played a crucial role in the evolution of architectural forms, since the time of the ancient Babylonians. Weights and measurements have been and remain necessary components in the study of every area of human nature and natural phenomena, from the development of fashion, to the distribution of food and supplies, to the exploration of planets.

Using a theme to approach curriculum study is no more nor less than what the creative educator does spontaneously at one time or another in the classroom. Using the arts as both central focus and connection to all subject areas, however, enables every teacher to systematize the approach for use at will.

> *"Literacy, in its richest, fullest sense, means communicating not just verbally, but nonverbally as well. Now more than ever, all people need to see clearly, hear acutely, and feel sensitively through the imagery of the arts. These skills are no longer just desirable; they are essential if we are to survive together with civility and joy. Without the capacity to extend the range of human expression to include music, dance, theater, the visual arts, and creative writing, students are crippled, just as surely as if they failed to learn to read and write."*

> *"Literacy in the Arts: An Imperative for New Jersey Schools." 1990.*

Determining the *central focus* of an arts-based thematic curriculum is the first step. This is initiated by the selection of a specific educational objective. Suppose the chosen objective is the exploration of the themes in a particular piece of literature. Relevant information to other subject areas may be extracted from that literary work and communicated by both traditional and arts-in-education strategies.

JACK AND THE BEANSTALK

An example of such activities from the primary language arts selection of "Jack and the Beanstalk" is given below:

In *Language Arts,* words from the story may be used for letter recognition (B - beans and beanstalk, C - cow, G - goose, giant, gold, etc.), for vocabulary, or even for simple subject-object-predicate sentence construction.

☺ *ACTIVITY: LETTER RECOGNITION.* Give each group of students a word from the story, e.g., "cow." They are to draw the starting letter on a piece of paper and hold it up while they act out the word.

Emphasizing that the story is an *English* folktale might generate interest in other English folktales such as "Tom Thumb," "Dick Whittington and His Cat," and "Jack the Giant-Killer."

At least three film versions of "Jack and the Beanstalk" are available on video cassette, starring respectively Mickey Mouse, Abbott and Costello, and Gene Kelly.

In *Visual and Performing Arts,* the story offers a natural introduction to harp music and a comparison of styles of book illustrations (since, as with most popular children's stories, there exists a wide variety of illustrative interpretations).

☺ *ACTIVITY: RECOGNIZING INSTRUMENTS.* Play some examples of harp music for your students. See if they recognize the instrument. Show them pictures of modern-day and ancient harps.

☺ *ACTIVITY: PICTURE STATUES.* Find different illustration styles for the story and break the children into groups. Give each group a different style picture (ideally of the same moment or subject in the story) and have them make a statue of the picture. They can become human or inanimate objects. Then have them prepare and act out the action which immediately precedes the picture, so their scene ends up in a freeze of the picture.

Acting out the story offers the learning of theater games, pantomime and improvisation, as well as design and construction of scenery, costumes and stage properties.

In *Science,* the principles of giantism, vegetables, nutrition, growth cycles, photosynthesis, cows, geese, and animal husbandry are all treated in the story and may logically lead to further exploration and study. Even an introduction to clouds and weather may be approached, because the giant's castle is "in the clouds."

☺ *ACTIVITY: WEATHER.* How might the story be changed if it were either raining or a clear day? Have students act out the story with different options for the weather, i.e., it is raining, or it is a clear day and there are no clouds (good creative problem solving example for Gifted and Talented students).

In *Mathematics,* opportunities exist for thematic integration in the recognition of numbers: the number 3 figures prominently in the story: 3 magic beans, in some versions; 3 objects Jack steals from the giant (a bag of gold, the goose that laid the golden egg, and the singing harp); 3 characters at the beginning of the story (Jack, his mother and the cow).

☺ *ACTIVITY: ACTING WORD PROBLEMS*. Have your students create statues of the number 3 with their bodies (see *Statue Game*, variations, p.35). Act out word problems in which the number 3 figures prominently. For example, Jack has three cows and he trades one cow for three beans. How many beans and cows does he have now?

The use of money and bartering may also be explored. (What is the relative monetary worth of a cow and a handful of beans, and their by-products)?

In *History/Social Studies,* symbol recognition (money, music, up, down, and clouds, for instance), the concepts of buying, selling, and bartering, various occupations, different social classes, and the socio-psychological effects of hunger are all inherent in the story.

☺ *ACTIVITY: VOCABULARY GAME*. Acting out vocabulary words can test students' understandings of meaning. Break students into groups. Give each group a list of words. Each group is to choose one word from their list. They are to act it out in pantomime. Other groups (the audience) are to confer quietly and write down their guess as to what the word is. After checking each audience group's guess, find out what the acting group was doing. Score, if you wish: one point for each audience group which guessed correctly, and as many points for the acting group as there were audience groups guessing correctly. You may also wish to put on the board a list of all the words which audience groups may refer to when guessing.

Setting the story in medieval times (its traditional setting) adds possibilities for the study of marketplaces, guilds, and medieval social structures.

In *Physical Education,* English folk dances (such as villagers might perform after the giant is killed), rope climbing (as a kinetic simulation of what Jack experienced climbing a beanstalk), the physical effects of proper and improper nutrition, and medieval games such as blindman's bluff and ring-around-a-rosy may effectively complement the study of the story itself.

As for behavioral objectives, "Jack and the Beanstalk," like all myths, legends, folktales and fairy tales (each was originally a *teaching* story) is abundant in questions of ethics, logic, morality, faith, and service.

LIFE IN ANCIENT GREECE

A somewhat different approach may be taken for a History-Social Studies objective. Let's examine the process of designing an arts-based thematic curriculum unit on "Life in Ancient Greece." These are the steps:

Step 1. Select a central focus from a piece of core literature of or about the period. We selected the myth of Demeter and Persephone for three reasons:
   a. Because it is one of the most often repeated stories in Greek mythology.
   b. The poet Homer thought this myth important enough for him to compose an ode about it, comparable in literary merit to his "Iliad" and "Odyssey."

c. The myth of Demeter and Persephone formed the basis of a significant mystery school in Eleusis and played an important role in Greek religion.

Step 2. Identify the themes in the story: The more relevant themes in Demeter and Persephone include:
a. Relationships of Greek gods to the natural world and each other.
b. The concepts of fertility; agriculture; the relationship between cosmic law, psychological needs and material considerations; justice and mercy; death and resurrection; and the cycle of seasons.
c. The universal principle often expressed as "every action causes an equal and opposite reaction."

Step 3. Determine how each curriculum area may suggest thematic content relative to the themes identified: The Olympic games and the pentathlon; the Greek alphabet and English words derived from the Greek; plays and theater; pottery, sculpture and architecture; agriculture and botany; the contributions of the ancient Greeks to the fields of astronomy, physics, mathematics, geometry, and philosophy; geography, social customs, and history of ancient Greece are all viable areas of study derived from this one Greek myth.

Step 4. Relate each area of study to the central focus - the literary piece. A particularly effective way to do this is through the collective creation of a work of art. A mural, a model city of Athens, or a dramatization of the story are examples. This crystallizes the experience for the students and gives objective and immediate relevance to information received. Thus, rather than being motivated by the desire to get good grades and pass tests, students are motivated by the desire to express their creativity--certainly a more inspirational, and probably a more worthy, motivation.

The process of designing an arts-based thematic curriculum is simple and fun. The teaching of such a curriculum is a challenge, and the reward is, for both teacher and students, a total educational experience.

"The value of the arts in the total education of the child is significant and can be positively evaluated."

"Evaluating the Arts in Education: A Responsive Approach." 1975.

CURRICULUM WHEEL - JACK AND THE BEANSTALK

CURRICULUM WHEEL - LIFE IN ANCIENT GREECE

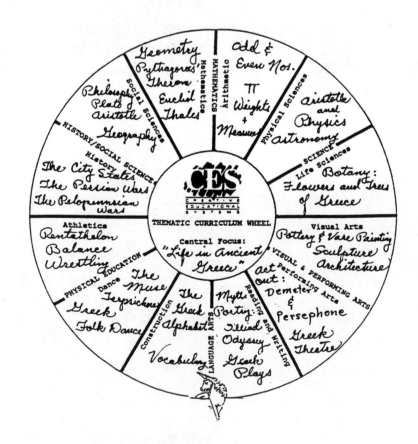

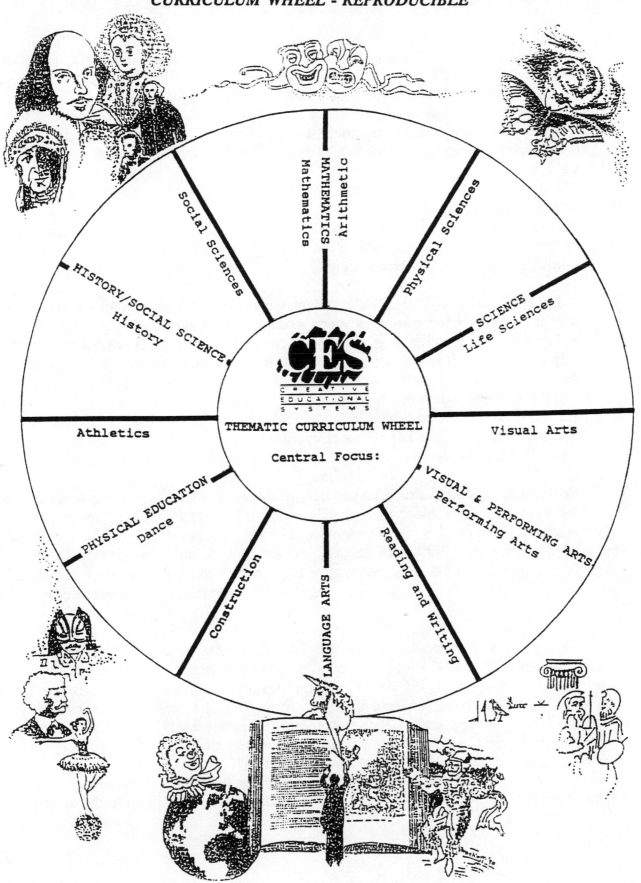

MATHEMATICS
Arithmetic

Social Sciences

Physical Sciences

HISTORY/SOCIAL SCIENCE
History

SCIENCE
Life Sciences

CES
CREATIVE
EDUCATIONAL
SYSTEMS

Athletics

THEMATIC CURRICULUM WHEEL

Central Focus:

Visual Arts

PHYSICAL EDUCATION
Dance

VISUAL & PERFORMING ARTS
Performing Arts

Construction

LANGUAGE ARTS

Reading and Writing

THE THEATRICALIZATION OF NON-DRAMATIC MATERIAL

Anything can be dramatized. Plays have been created out of scripture ("Godspell"), poems ("Cats"), interviews ("A Chorus Line"), court records ("Inherit the Wind"), comic strips ("Lil' Abner", "Superman"), and paintings ("Sunday in the Park with George"), not to mention short stories, novels, biographies, historical events, or sheer flights of fancy.

In order to turn a piece of non-dramatic material into a play, it is necessary to first identify three primary components of drama: setting, character, and plot. *Setting* identifies both the "where" and the "when" of a situation; *character* identifies the "who;" and *plot,* the "what" and "how."

"Why," of course, is the *theme,* which may be described as the message being communicated, the moral, or the educational objective.

Setting is where the action takes place. A specific setting helps both actors and audience members to immediately relate to their place in a scene intellectually. It can also establish a mood to which they may relate emotionally:

☺ *ACTIVITY: SETTING IMPROV.* Give students a list of environments: an office, a woods, a castle, a living room, a street, a courtroom, or even an empty space. Ask them to add descriptive words to each setting to create a mood or an emotional reaction. You might get such responses as a *busy* newspaper office; an *enchanted* woods; a *dark and ruined* castle; a *comfortable, middle-class family living* room; a *deserted* street; a *shabby, small-town* courtroom; or a *brightly-lit* empty space. (For the creation of scenery to give the illusion of these and other environments, see *"The Elements of Scene Design,"* p.122). Next have them act out the environment non-verbally while the class attempts to guess the descriptive word they chose.

Setting involves time also. Time of day, historical period, or even a specific date will clarify the environment in which the dramatic action is to occur. Consider, for example, the different situations implied in the "shabby, small-town courtroom" scene if it is placed in Tennessee, in the early 1930's, in August, at nine o'clock on a Monday morning; or in Tombstone, Arizona in 1895, on a hot muggy afternoon; or in Philadelphia, on July 3, 1776. The more the imagination of actors and audiences is stimulated, *the more successful your production is likely to be.*

Characters may be people, of course; or animals, personifications of ideals or principles, or even inanimate objects. The medieval morality play "Everyman" contains characters such as Pride, Wealth, Hope, and Good Works. Maurice Maeterlinck's marvelous Christmas fantasy "The Blue Bird" includes, as characters, Light, Sugar, Bread, Fire, Night, and even different varieties of trees, in one scene. Native American legends personify not only animals, but vegetables, fruits, grains, weather conditions and the natural elements, even constellations in the heavens. (For the development of characters, please see *"Characterization,"* p.83).

With characters as with setting, the more specific you can be, the more fun your students will have portraying their roles and the clearer the communication will be to the audience.

☺ *ACTIVITY: CHARACTER WALK.* Choose a student to walk around in front of the class (on stage) as a princess would walk. A character simply described as "a princess" does not give an actor (student or professional) much to work with. Ask the student-actor to now walk as a "vain and haughty princess;" as a "vain and haughty princess who is a glutton;" and finally as all of the above and add that she is "looking for a husband." Such a character is one any actor can sink his or her teeth into. Have another student walk around or perform a series of simple actions (like washing dishes, preparing a meal, making a bed, etc.) as Gepetto, from the story of "Pinocchio." By those directions you give, emphasize that Gepetto is not merely an "old man"; rather he is better identified as "a kind and gentle old man who is a lonely woodcarver and longs for a son." In each example you choose, have the class note how characterization and movement changes as you become more specific about who the character is.

Whereas specific settings establish locality and mood, specific characters generate interest. The more complex an actor makes a character, the more he will learn about human nature in preparing to play a role, and the more the audience will be involved in watching and listening to what happens to the characters. The popular success of TV sitcoms, soap operas, and even cartoons is based on the adventures of *interesting* characters.

Plot, most simply stated, is the story: a sequence of events with a beginning, a middle, and an end.

The beginning (whether represented by narration, dialogue, pantomimed action, or any combination thereof) establishes 1) where and when the action is taking place, 2) who is involved, and 3) what the situation is as the play opens.

If, as audience members, we see a little girl with golden curls creep through the door of a cottage in the woods, look around cautiously and suddenly notice a large chair, a medium-sized chair, and a small chair, we are psychologically prepared to accept whatever will happen next. If a narrator tells us that during the Civil War, three young Confederate infantrymen were the sole survivors of a battle and became lost in the woods, but we then see them eating, drinking, and singing around a campfire, we will be eager to watch and listen. If a king is discovered in his private chambers complaining to his most trusted courtiers that the Palace Treasury is empty and that his daughter refuses to marry any of her wealthy suitors because she is in love with a penniless poet, we are both intellectually and emotionally involved in the story within the first few minutes.

The middle of any play is that part of the story which introduces and develops the *conflict.* Conflict is that element of opposing ideas, events, or character desires which create the dramatic action. After Goldilocks goes to sleep, the three bears enter the cottage. The three Confederate infantrymen encounter a wounded, black Union soldier. The king's palace is visited by a masked knight, etc. The middle of a play is the gist of a story, most often described by a student when asked, "What was the story about?"

The ending of a play usually resolves the conflict presented in the middle. Goldilocks runs away and the three bears settle down into their normal routine. The three Confederate infantrymen agree to risk their lives to take the wounded Union soldier back to his family up North, across enemy lines. The masked knight is revealed to be the penniless poet loved by the princess, they marry and live happily ever after.

A play does not have to have a happy ending, but it does have to have an ending in order to satisfy the emotional and intellectual needs of the audience who have become involved in the story. The success of movie serials, mini-series and episodic TV shows is based on the audience's psychological need for a conclusion. The audience will keep watching, seeking a resolution.

GUIDELINES FOR THEATRICALIZATION

Following are guidelines for theatricalizing (or dramatizing) various kinds of non-dramatic materials relevant to classroom study.

I. Literature

A. Divide the story (or portion of the story you are dramatizing) into scenes, each with its own specific *setting*. For example, for *The Wizard of Oz*:

Scene 1:   a farmhouse in turn-of-the-century Kansas;
Scene 2:   Munchkinland;
Scene 3:   the yellow-brick road;
Scene 4:   a field of poppies;
Scene 5:   the gates of the Emerald City, etc.

B. Determine which *characters* will be in each scene:

Scene 1:   Dorothy, Toto, Uncle Henry and Aunt Em.
Scene 2:   Dorothy, Toto, Glinda the Good, the Munchkins, and the Wicked Witch of the West.
Scene 3:   Dorothy, Toto, the Scarecrow, the Tin Woodsman, and the Cowardly Lion, etc.

C. Determine the *sequence of events* which will occur in each scene. Scenario:

Scene 1:   1) Dorothy expresses discontent with her life in Kansas and longs for adventure;
2) a cyclone threatens and everyone runs for shelter;
3) Toto runs into the farmhouse, Dorothy follows him and the house is carried away by the cyclone, etc.

♪ *NOTE:* For poems or essays, setting, characters and/or sequences of events may have to be created by you and your students to illustrate the concept or theme presented. This part of the process might well provide for several classes of enjoyable improvisation and learning in and of itself.

II. Historical Events

A. Divide the event into different scenes and establish settings for each one, e.g.,
Scene 1: The Green Dragon Tavern in Boston, where colonists gather to complain about British tyranny;
Scene 2: Outside the Green Dragon, where John Hancock and Sam Adams tell Paul Revere they must leave town and enlist his cooperation in warning them when the British begin an attack;
Scene 3: The road to Lexington and Concord where Paul will ride.
B. Determine which characters will appear in each scene, just as with literature, above.

C. List the sequence of events in each scene with as much detail as possible, again as with literature, above (this constitutes the *scenario*).

III. **Biographies, Representations of Different Cultures, and Scientific Concepts** may be approached in the same manner as described above. Examples:

A. Biography of Harriet Tubman. A scenario:

Scene 1:	Harriet is discovered as a young woman arguing with her mother that there is a better way to to live than in slavery.
Scene 2:	She is next seen escaping to the North with the help of the Underground Railroad.
Scene 3:	Harriet, at an abolitionist meeting, decides to rescue her parents, and so on.

B. Chinese Culture, the T'ang Dynasty. A scenario:

Scene 1:	A Chinese boy and girl decide to run away from their farm work.
Scene 2:	They go to the fair in the marketplace of a nearby large city.
Scene 3:	They meet a magician who allows them to experience apprenticeship with different kinds of merchants.
Scene 4:	They save a noble lady from a runaway horse.
Scene 5:	She invites them to be her guests at a feast in court.

C. The Scientific Concept of Cycles. A scenario:

Scene 1:	An actor comes on stage as the sun, arms outstretched, "radiating warmth and light."
Scene 2:	Other actors appear, each representing a different planet, each personifying the planet's distinguishing characteristics.
Scene 3:	Actor-planets revolve around the Sun, moving with different speeds to illustrate the movement relationships of different planets.

D. The Scientific Concept of the Seasons. A scenario:

Scene 1:	Actors enter as seeds, kneel, and cover their heads.
Scene 2:	Other actors, interacting as characterizations of rain and sunlight, pass over the seeds.
Scene 3:	The actor-seeds develop into plants by unfolding and rising, their hands reaching up toward the sky.
Scene 4:	An actor portraying the sun comes out and the plants grow further.
Scene 5:	An actor portraying the wind comes and the plants sway and shiver.
Scene 6:	A new actor, portraying snow, comes out and interacts with the plants, which shrivel and collapse.
Scene 7:	The rain and sun come back. Seeds begin to grow again.

Once you have selected the material you wish to dramatize, and have followed the procedure of determining setting, character, and plot, you will have created a scenario. After that, it remains but to develop a script (p.78), rehearse the script as a play (p.93), and add scenery, costumes, properties, lighting, and sound, as desired.

This process is much simpler than it may seem upon first reading; and once completed successfully, becomes easier each time it is followed, until it becomes naturally intuitive.

Try it. You'll like it!

"The benefit to be gained from programs infusing the arts into general education include increased awareness and appreciation of the environment, attention to mutual needs, ability to experiment and create, and satisfactions intrinsic to total involvement. Achievement of such benefits leads to increased effectiveness of an overall educational program which has as its goal a high quality education for each individual."

> *"Report of the Ad Hoc Committee for Integrating the Arts into General Education." 1977.*

THE VITAL IMPORTANCE OF CLEAR OBJECTIVES

All art forms are neutral in essence. Dance, music, poetry, drama, and the visual arts may be utilized to communicate any content desired. When used as teaching strategies, therefore, it is vital that specific learning objectives be identified if the arts-in-education lessons you teach are to have the greatest possible impact.

"To teach a class about the American Revolution" is not a clear objective. "To have students *understand* the primary and secondary causes of the revolution" is more specific. "To allow your students to *experience the feelings* of unfair restrictions and the oppression which led the colonists to rebel" is an even clearer objective; and one which may be powerfully communicated through the arts.

Simply stated, the arts may be used as a right-brain method to communicate left-brain information. This method works because the arts affect the senses, the emotions, and the body, as well as the mind. It is up to you, the educator, to supply the content.

CURRICULUM OBJECTIVES

Regardless of what curriculum unit you are approaching, it is possible to teach it effectively through the arts.

☺ *ACTIVITY: CLOUD FORMATIONS.* Describe different kinds of clouds and have students give their own movement interpretations of each type.

☺ *ACTIVITY: GEOMETRY ART.* Have students create their own geometric designs and transfer them onto silk-screened T-shirts.

☺ *ACTIVITY: VOCABULARY AND SENTENCE STRUCTURE.* Use the theater game described above (p.64) for vocabulary; vary it by using parts of speech instead of vocabulary words to teach sentence structure.

☺ *ACTIVITY: POINTS OF VIEW IN THE CIVIL WAR.* Teach conflicting sentiments of the North and the South in the Civil War by studying songs and music of the period.

The possibilities are endless. A student may learn more about the French and Indian Wars from studying the costumes, weapons, and tactics of both sides and then role-playing and reenacting a battle than by any amount of lecture and textbook study.

Algebraic equations taught through rap music; the study of plants through writing poetry; even the understanding of great literature by pantomiming the actions of the characters may help your students learn more fully, more completely, more meaningfully.

First: Choose the specific unit objective you wish to teach.

Second: Determine the art form which you would like to use as a teaching strategy.

Third: Engage your students in the arts activity, making sure they understand the learning objective.

Fourth: Evaluate with your students the effectiveness of the lesson.

You say you are unfamiliar with the techniques of the various art forms? That's all right. So are your students, probably. Refer to the *Elements of Creativity* (p.48). Hire an artist-in-residence. Try doing the arts activity yourself. It is the *creative process* which is important here, rather than the striving towards a finished product. Who's going to criticize you? Your students? ...or yourself?

BEHAVIORAL OBJECTIVES ♥

Depending on the objective and the particular art form, the nature of arts activities contain behavioral objectives inherent within them. Self-esteem, critical thinking, cooperation, the expression of emotions, responsibility, and tolerance may each be communicated with potency through the arts, whether the activity be directed to a curriculum objective, or specifically toward behavior modification.

Points of emphasis in working with behavioral objectives include:

1. Praise each child for their efforts, regardless of the results. (For example, "Did you notice how well Manuel listened to the other actors in that scene?")

2. Direct your student's attention to the specific learning objective before the activity begins. (For example, "In order to be able to do this together, you're really going to have to cooperate!")

3. Point out how students deal with the objective throughout the process. ("Table One is really cooperating in the planning of their scene.")

4. At the end of the activity, evaluate with your students (through writing or discussion) the success in accomplishing the learning objective. (For example, "Did this scene show us how to cooperate on the playground? How did it do that?")

THE GAME OF BUILDING A CIVILIZATION

This activity has been used successfully with groups from fourth grade through adult. In addition to its more obvious educational objectives (such as self-discipline, non-verbal communication, and group cooperation), it also teaches the basis of the underlying unity between all peoples, without relying on any doctrine, philosophy, or belief system. It is an example of experiential education in its purest form. It is included here as an example of an activity which will not only powerfully emphasize a number of behavioral objectives, but will, as well, provide a framework for numerous language arts and/or social studies objectives.

1. Divide the class into three relatively equal groups.

2. Place each group in a different part of the room.

3. *Privately,* give each group a simple objective. Make sure no one hears the objective of any group other than their own:
    Group I: "Defend your territory.
    Group II: "Build a place of worship."
    Group III: "Create a shelter."

4. There are only three rules to the game. Each, however, is very important.
    a. Keep the activity non-verbal. Sounds and gestures may be used, but no words.
    b. Anything in the room may be used, but at the first indication of potential harm to any person or property, the activity will be halted. Also, at the conclusion, everything must be returned as it was before the game started.
    c. Everyone must continue to play the game until the teacher-director stops it. It is recommended that the activity be continued at least 25-30 minutes. This will give the players time to run out of pre-judged activities, go through an inevitable but brief time of boredom, and begin to respond spontaneously to one another.

After the game is over and the room is restored to order (which should be done quickly and quietly) it is helpful to lead a group discussion on the players' perceptions of their own behavior and the behavior of the others.

Because this game deals with primal objectives, without the sophisticated mask of language, players of any age are inevitably surprised at their emotional responses and usually gain startling insights into basic, human behavior patterns.

This is an excellent activity to introduce a period in ancient history, or to prepare for the study of major social concepts, such as war, patriotism, or religious evangelism.

"One definition of 'work' is 'play with purpose.'"

WTS

AM I TEACHING ALL MY CHILDREN?
A Learning Modalities Evaluation

A synthesis of visual and performing arts experiences, carefully planned and regularly monitored, will communicate effectively to all learning modalities. Below is a set of evaluation standards, using Howard Gardner's "Theory of Multiple Intelligences," as described in his book *Frames of Mind*. Regardless of what multiple-intelligence paradigm is used, however, what follows is a handy reference guide to self-evaluation in teaching methodology.

Learning Modality	*Evaluation Standards*
Linguistic:	Is the language used during this unit semantically understood and correctly used? Are students gaining a richer appreciation of and expression in their native tongue? Am I learning to master the use of language as a teaching tool?
Logical-Mathematical:	Is the sequence of unit components clear and orderly? Can students follow the logic of the unit's organization of information? Is the pattern of my method structure as effective as I want it to be at this time?
Spatial:	Do the visual experiences in this unit communicate the content transmitted? Are students aware of and able to use visual aesthetic principles in their communication? Am I consciously using effective visual cues in my presentations?
Musical:	Is the music to which students are exposed during this unit appropriate in mood, imagery, and style to the content being taught? Are students able to relate musical form to their receipt of information? Am I choosing musical selections which reinforce concepts inherent in curriculum objectives?
Body-Kinesthetic:	Are physical experiences engaging both the tactile sense and motor skills integrated into this curriculum unit? Do students move with confidence in their curriculum-oriented, body-kinesthetic activities? Am I using my body to model experiences for my students?
Interpersonal:	Is this curriculum unit designed to give students the opportunity to dialogue, both with me and with one another, about what they are learning? Are students openly asking questions and expressing their opinions about the unit content? Am I being honest in expressing what I think, what I feel, what I know, and what I don't know?

Intrapersonal: Does the unit content relate directly to the students' lives? Do the students recognize and acknowledge what they are learning about themselves through the study of unit subject matter? Am I consistently teaching from my life experiences? and am I gaining new insights about my life experience through what I am teaching?

Not only do children have multiple intelligences. So do teachers. Thus it is incumbent on the teacher to develop each of his or her modalities of learning in order to wholly teach each child.

"One grows by helping others. And one helps others by growing."

WTS

CHAPTER FIVE

CREATING A PLAY

"To me it seems as if when God conceived the world, that was Poetry; He formed it, and that was Sculpture; He colored it, and that was Painting; He peopled it with living beings, and that was the grand, divine, eternal Drama."

Charlotte Cushman

The difference between an improvisation and a play is the difference between a sketch and a finished painting, between a jam session and a musical composition.

A play is a structured work of dramatic art. To act in a well-constructed play is to experience the richness of language, the emotional content of a well-told story, the actions and reactions of dimensional characters, the sweep of precisely-crafted dramatic action and the confidence of carefully creating an illusion which will intellectually, emotionally, and sensorially involve an audience.

Much of what is considered the world's great literature is in dramatic form. To be culturally literate, all students should have the opportunity to learn experientially how to create such a form and how to bring it into living expression as a shared communal experience.

This chapter is about how to create a play.

"Arts education should provide all students with a sense of the arts in civilization, of creativity in the artistic process, of the vocabularies of artistic communication and of the critical elements necessary to making informed choices about the products of the arts."

"Toward Civilization"
National Endowment for the Arts

DEVELOPING A SCRIPT

A play is different than any other form of literature in that a story is told primarily through dialogue. Dialogue is essentially conversation between two or more people.

The opening dialogue of a play is called *exposition*. Exposition explains the situation to the audience. Often, a narrator is used for this purpose. For example:

Narrator: Long, long ago, in a city far, far away, lived a boy named Aladdin. Aladdin, I'm sorry to say, though he was strong, good-looking, and intelligent, was a lazy, good-for-nothing boy who spent his days hanging around the streets of the city with equally ne'er-do-well companions, while his poor, widowed mother worked day and night to make a living for herself and her worthless son. One day, however, Aladdin's life changed suddenly, when a mysterious stranger confronted him in the street and claimed to be his long, lost uncle...

The narrator, as a dramatic device to set a scene, is not always necessary. In the above example, the same information might be conveyed simply through dialogue and stage directions (which we'll get to later). For example:

(Scene: ALADDIN is discovered on a street corner playing a gambling game with a group of other teenage boys. So engrossed in the game are they, that they fail to notice a mysterious robed STRANGER who enters quietly and watches them intently as they play.)

MOTHER: (Calling off) Aladdin!

(The boys stop playing and look up, apprehensively. The STRANGER slides into the shadows and continues watching).

MOTHER: (off) Aladdin! Where are you, you young scalawag? Aladdin!!

ALADDIN: (To the boys) Quick! Hide! If she catches me gambling, I'll be in more trouble than I already am!

(The boys, including ALADDIN, quickly scamper behind boxes and baskets as MOTHER enters.)

MOTHER: Oh, Aladdin, if your father were still alive, he'd beat you within an inch of your life for leaving your poor mother to work her fingers to the bone just to keep a roof over our heads and food on the table. Look at me! I've got bony fingers! How can I weave beautiful cloth with bony fingers? (turning her eyes skyward) You *would* beat him, wouldn't you, Mustapha? No, you probably wouldn't. You never did while you were alive, and look how he turned out! Aladdin! Where are you? I can't do everything myself! There's wool to buy, and cloth to sell, and garments to sew, and food to prepare... Aladdin! You come home this minute!

(She exits, calling for her son. ALADDIN and the other boys emerge from their hiding places).

ALADDIN: (Somewhat abashed) She does go on and on, doesn't she?

(The STRANGER steps out of the shadows to within a few feet behind ALADDIN. The other boys see him and, frightened, back away quietly and then make a rapid exit).

ALADDIN: Hey, where are you going? It's all right! She won't be back this way for another half hour! Achmed! Casmir?

(Puzzled at their hasty retreat, ALADDIN scratches his head and turns around, finding himself confronting the STRANGER. The STRANGER smiles broadly and throws his arms around the boy).

STRANGER: Nephew!

ALADDIN: (Startled, he quickly disentangles himself from the STRANGER's embrace). Uh, who, me?

STRANGER: You're Aladdin, aren't you?

ALADDIN: Yes,... er, I mean, why?

STRANGER: And your father was Mustapha the weaver, right?

ALADDIN: Tailor.

STRANGER: Tailor. Your mother is the weaver, right?

ALADDIN: (Still suspicious) Right.

STRANGER: (Embracing him again) Nephew!

ALADDIN: (Breaking free) Stop that! Who are you?

STRANGER: Dear boy, I am your uncle! Long, lost brother to your dear, departed father, Mustapha! And I'm back! Back from the jungles of Africa where I discovered the treasures of lost civilizations. Back with more gold and precious gems than I could ever use in one lifetime. Back to see that my dear brother's son gets the wealth and position he deserves. It's me, Aladdin! I've come back -- to make you and your mother rich beyond your wildest dreams!

ALADDIN: (embracing the STRANGER) Uncle!

STRANGER: (returning the embrace) Nephew! Now, why don't you take me to meet your mother so that we can all begin our new lives.

(They exit, arm-in-arm, as the boys creep silently on and look at one another in wonder).

An exposition scene in dialogue may take longer, but generally it's more interesting, more emotionally involving.

How, then, to write dialogue so that it sounds like real people having a real conversation? Professional playwrights listen to people talking. Often, they will carry a notebook with them and jot down interesting snatches of dialogue which they hear in a supermarket or on a street corner. They may later incorporate this into a scene.

If your students are skilled in improvisation (see p.30), have them improvise a scene and record it on a pocket tape recorder and then transcribe the dialogue on paper. Or have several groups work on the dialogue for each scene in the *scenario* (see p.71) and read them to the class. Let the class decide which lines sound most natural and tell the story most effectively.

If, on the other hand, you determine to improvise the dialogue from the scenario, take care that all the important plot elements (incidents and ideas) are covered in each scene of the play. After rehearsing several times, certain lines will most likely become standard in each scene and a "script" will evolve naturally.

Opening lines and closing lines for a scene deserve special consideration (see *First Line/Last Line Improvs,* p.38) Usually, an opening line should strongly convey the immediate situation. For example,

"Now, Sheng, you must take care of your sisters while I take this basket of goodies to your grandmother. And don't open the door to anyone while I'm gone."

or

"Tom, I just can't go any further. We've been walking through this awful old cave for hours and we still don't know where we are. We're lost, Tom, we're lost!"

or

"Listen to this item in today's newspaper! King George has just issued a proclamation declaring that he's putting a tax on all the English tea coming into Boston Harbor!"

Opening lines like these generate a response and prepare the way for moving the story forward through more dialogue.

A closing line to a scene is comparable to a punctuation mark at the end of a sentence. It essentially lets the audience know the scene is over *and* there is more to come (except for the final scene, of course. The end of a play should let everyone know the story is finished). For example,

"Oh, mother, I'm so glad you're home! But sit down now, and let us tell you what happened to Lon Po Po."

or

"Look, Becky, it's a light! Come on, Becky, you can make it! Just a little further and we'll be saved!"

or

"Ready, boys? War paint on? Tomahawks ready? Then, let's holler all the way to Boston Harbor and strike a blow for freedom!"

Few things are more disconcerting for an audience than to be unsure when a scene begins or ends.

STAGE DIRECTIONS

Stage directions are traditionally set off by parentheses and *never* spoken by the actors. They describe, in as brief terms as possible, the major physical actions taken by the characters during the course of the play. Stage directions may also give the description of the setting, e.g.,

(The interior of a small cottage. There is a fire burning in a stone fireplace, a deserted loom in the corner, and a table set for two. It is mid-afternoon.)

Primary stage movements of a character are also indicated by stage directions, e.g.,

(Ivan tiptoes across the empty room, looks around nervously and slips a letter under the clock on the mantlepiece.)

A particular emotional quality the actor needs to give to a certain line may be given through a stage direction, e.g.,

Sarah: (Petulantly) Do we have to go to school again, today?

Stage directions, when used imaginatively, give a scene dramatic tension and expanded levels of meaning, and provide a general guideline for actors as to what to do with their bodies and voices while delivering their lines.

The major requisites of the *form* of a script are:
  1) that it is clear which character is speaking;
  2) that stage directions are set apart from the dialogue;
  3) that there is enough room on the script for an actor to write down his or her blocking and make notes.

Please see *Sample Script Page* on p. 104.

Perhaps the best way to learn to write scripts is to read them--as many as you can, as often as you have time. Please see *Appendix C* for a selected list of plays which are suitable for school presentation and which are fun to read.

GUIDELINES FOR CASTING

A famous actress, Ellen Terry, once remarked, "The three most difficult things about acting are concentration, concentration, and concentration."

The same might be said about any creative endeavor, from painting a picture to preparing a superb dinner.

In acting, concentration is focused in three areas: listening, staying in character, and telling the story.

Concentration on listening is necessary in order to follow directions and to respond appropriately to fellow actors. Improvisation is thus an excellent listening activity.

Concentration on staying in character is necessary to maintain the illusion of "reality" for the audience. If a character is supposed to be frightened and the actor begins to giggle, for example, the illusion is broken. Sometimes student actors will give excellent performances in a scene and then "break" character as they are exiting, thus spoiling the effect they have created. "Stay in character until you're offstage," and "Get into character before you enter," are two of most often repeated directions given to student actors.

"Telling the story" requires concentration because the actor must create the appropriate mood for each scene in order to stimulate the desired emotional response from the audience. Nearly every story has expository passages, lyrical moments, scenes of suspense, "foreshadowing" of what's going to be happening next, moments of climax, etc. A play does this almost entirely through dialogue and quality of movement. To keep the audience relating to what's being communicated, then, requires quite a bit of concentration on the part of an actor.

In casting, therefore, look for the ability to concentrate, especially in the major roles. Good readers are often good at concentration, as are those students who are good at sports, crafts, or simply listening and following directions.

Type casting is unavoidable to some degree. To have the largest girl in the class paired with the smallest boy as a romantic team is likely to stimulate a reaction from the audience which will be something other than romantic. To cast a shy boy as a dashing hero, regardless of how right he may look for the part, may be asking for more work than you have time for.

And to cast the class clown in a role in which he has to primarily give focus onstage to what's going on between other actors, is virtually begging for trouble.

On the other hand, girls can often play men's roles (the opposite rarely applies in our contemporary culture). Sometimes a student who is inept at academic skills will shine on stage. The shy boy may be astonishingly expressive when he takes on a role. The extroverted girl may freeze up when she finds herself in the spotlight. And the class clown may be a budding star, just waiting for a chance to channel all that energy.

Warm-up theater games and activities should, over a period of time, give insight into who will be right for what in the drama experience, but you never know. Prepare to be surprised.

It *is* true that "there are no small parts, only small actors," if you'll forgive the pun.

Trying to explain this to the girl who is heartbroken because she didn't get to play the princess may be a challenge. Her role as a lady-in-waiting, however, is equally important to the telling of the story *and* she is playing a real character with thoughts and feelings and desires just as real as the character who has more lines, more time on stage and a prettier costume.

Watch a film or video with your class and discuss with them the supporting roles, i.e., actors with fewer lines and who appeared less often than the stars. How did these supporting players help to tell the story? What did they *do* which made them interesting to watch?

Aesop has taught us, "He who tries to please everyone, pleases no one."

In the matter of casting a play, please yourself.

CHARACTERIZATION

One of the main reasons acting appeals to so many young people is that it affords the opportunity to "play somebody else." In a dramatic role, one may escape one's normal behavior pattern for awhile and express attitudes, feelings, and ways of behaving which may be far different than the personality one demonstrates in everyday life.

"Playing house" is a popular game for very young children in which the little girl as "mother" often displays both more strictness as well as more gentleness than in ordinary activity. The boy playing "father" tends to display more independence (balanced with consideration of "mother's" needs) than is usual for him; and the child playing "the child" may be more undisciplined and less obedient than he is normally. Of course, the portrayal of these simple character traits will vary, depending on the role models of the players.

"Cops and robbers," "cowboys and Indians," professions like "nurse," "doctor," and "movie star," animal games, and "fairy princess" fantasies are other examples of play in which children naturally display characteristics which expand their imaginations and give them the opportunity to express qualities sometimes quite different than their everyday experience.

In creative drama, students often love to portray characters older or younger, richer or poorer, kinder or more wicked, stronger or weaker than themselves. In addition to allowing them to express traits which they may suppress in ordinary life, such play may help them to emotionally understand people who are different than they.

In order to enhance the dramatic experience of your students, as well as the quality of the performance, encourage them to give attention to *details* of characterization.

This activity may be as simple as getting a child to not only act out the movement and sounds of a particular animal, but to demonstrate the *kind* of animal they are playing. For example: Is the cat you're playing a *lazy* cat? A *ferocious* cat? A *suspicious* cat? A *stupid* cat? etc.

For older children, an examination of a character's unique qualities, their background, motivation, objectives, faults, virtues, and secrets will not only help them to better understand their characters, but will also provide a valuable experience in critical thinking.

CHARACTER ANALYSIS

Below are specific considerations for any character. Have each students answer these (either verbal or written) and then *show* how these considerations affect the character's behavior.

✓ **TIP:** The best response to the student's answer of "I don't know" (how a character walks, talks, thinks--whatever) is "Well, use your imagination. Make it up!"

✓ **TIP:** Having the student respond in the first person will help them *internalize* the character.

NAME
A character named Tyrone might display very different attributes from a character named Willie, for instance. A "Lizzie" might behave differently than an "Elizabeth."

☺ **ACTIVITY: MEANING OF NAMES.** Using a reference text or large dictionary, check out the meaning of character names.

AGE
Age differences are shown by changes in attitude, point of view and degrees of physical mobility.

☺ **ACTIVITY: AGE DIFFERENCES.** People move, speak and think differently at different ages. Have students discuss and demonstrate the difference between the way a child may respond to an argument and how a teenager might react... or an adult; the difference in movement between someone who is 50 years old and one who is 70; the way a child of 5 expresses disappointment; a child of 13; a 25-year-old.

OCCUPATION
A policeman is likely to take a different point of view in certain situations than will a doctor. A king or queen will probably move differently than a steel worker or a secretary. How does a person's work affect how they move, talk, and think?

☺ **ACTIVITY: OCCUPATIONS REVEALED.** Let students pick an occupation out of a hat (or choose one of their own). Have them come on stage in groups or singly and wait at a bus stop for a bus. They are to reveal through character traits what their occupation is. They are not to pantomime the work activity, e.g., a carpenter is not to pound nails; they are to imagine the person is not working and is waiting for the bus, e.g., a carpenter might have a sore shoulder and rub it. Stretch the image: add new elements to the imaginary situation. For example, after a few minutes, have them find out the bus is not coming and that there has been a large traffic accident which may prevent them from getting home for hours.

POSITION

A "boss" will demonstrate different characteristics from a "servant." The head of a family will act differently than the oldest child. Even a "queen" will tend to behave differently than a "princess." Have your students noticed any difference between a teacher and a principal? How does *position* affect a person's behavior?

☺ **ACTIVITY: CHARACTER POSITION.** Have students individually demonstrate the above differences by pantomiming a simple activity, such as walking into a room, or sitting down and picking up a sandwich from a nearby table, first as a boss, then as a servant; first as the head of the family, then as the oldest child; etc.

SECRET

Everyone has a private life which affects their attitudes toward different situations and, thereby, their behavior.

☺ **ACTIVITY: CHARACTER SECRET.** After assigning a character to each of your students, give them a character secret which they are to remember, but not reveal to the other players. Give them different situations to act out as their character.
Examples of secrets: "You're not really who you say you are," "You're afraid of high places," "You can't read or write," "You're a spy," "You're a visitor from another planet," etc.

A character secret does not have to be related to the story being acted out. Regardless of what it is, it will add dimension to the character which will be more interesting to the actor *and* the audience.

OBJECTIVE

The most important of all! Every character in a scene *wants* something. A king might want more power. A soldier may want to win the battle or avoid being killed. A mother may want to be left alone, or to be closer to her children, or to be obeyed. Characters who *want* different things create a conflict, which is the essence of drama.

☺ **ACTIVITY: OBJECTIVES.** Have students, working in pairs, each choose a character with an objective. Have them create improvisational scenes with a conflict. Have them redo the scene but take each aside and secretly change their objective. Note the difference in the way the scene is played.
Make sure students know what their characters want in every scene.

Most characters in plays are interesting because they live different lives than most of us. Your students can explore differences in motivation, lifestyle, and behavior. This will help them to become more tolerant, more compassionate, more understanding, and will give them a stronger sense of individuality.

Additional activities for helping young actors to develop strong characterization include:

☺ *ACTIVITY: CHARACTER PREFERENCES.* Write down a list of the character's likes and dislikes; favorite foods, colors, animals, hobbies, personal habits in others, subjects in school, relationships with family members and friends, daydreams, fears, desires, etc.

☺ *ACTIVITY: BIOGRAPHY.* Write a biography of the character.

☺ *ACTIVITY: HOT SEAT.* All players take turns sitting in a chair at the front of room, while the class asks them questions about their characters. The *character* (responding in the first person) does not have to answer truthfully, but must give *some* answer to every question.

☺ *ACTIVITY: SECRET IMPROV.* During recess or other individual or group activity, the player responds to whatever happens as their character, without being monitored by anyone. This can be great fun and can bring insights into a character which nothing else can. After allowing your students to try this (for from 10 minutes to half an hour), have them discuss what they experienced and what they learned about their characters.

☺ *ACTIVITY: POINT OF VIEW.* Have the students write the story they are dramatizing from the point of view of the character they are playing. Red Riding Hood, the Wolf, the Grandmother and the Hunter, for instance, will each undoubtedly tell quite a different story about the same event.

Developing a character is fun. It's a way of learning a lot about many subjects and, at the same time, creating a better play.

"(Art is) the only substitute for what we ourselves have not experienced."

Aleksandr Solzhenitsyn
Nobel Lecture, 1972

ORAL INTERPRETATION: READING ALOUD WITH MEANING

The human voice is a magnificent instrument, capable of communicating myriad sounds, amazing gradations of emotional expression, and a range of volumes from the slightest whisper to a mighty roar. Like any other communicating part of our organism, however, the voice must be trained in order to communicate meaning effectively.

Reading aloud is an inherent part of any language arts curriculum from the very first reading lesson through high school graduation. Emphasis, however, is put almost exclusively on proper pronunciation and enunciation and occasionally on volume. Reading with meaning, when encouraged, is generally so slight as to be almost unrecognizable--only brief pauses at commas and periods or a rising inflection at question marks. The occasional student who may be captured by the beauty and power of the language, or even caught up with the power of emotional content, learns at an early age that reading with *too much* meaning is "not cool" with peers and neither rewarded nor encouraged by the teacher.

Thus it is that when a student is asked to narrate a story, or recite a poem, or read dialogue from a play, too often the results are neither aesthetically pleasing, emotionally moving, nor intellectually stimulating. Like so much else in the classroom, reading aloud becomes an unwelcome task rather than a creative opportunity.

Following are a few simple but effective principles and exercises which, if followed and applied, will greatly improve your students' ability to read aloud and possibly their interest in reading. In many of the activities in oral interpretation, students will be required to work with a speech they are familiar with. One of the first preparations you can make is:

☺ **ACTIVITY: ORAL INTERPRETATION.** Assign, or have the students choose, a speech of one half to one minute in length which they are to memorize. Have them read it aloud. Tape and save their first reading, if possible, so that they may monitor their progress.

PHRASING

Generally, we do not speak in complete sentences, but rather in phrases. To translate the written word into the spoken word, have your students work on a phrase at a time, each with its own meaning, each to be expressed in its own way.

☺ **ACTIVITY: PHRASING.** Use a recorder, or alternatively a video camera, if available. If not, do this activity in front of the class. Have an individual read the following sentence while the class observes and you record:

"Once upon a time, deep in the forests of a distant land, there lived an old woman who was very lonely."

There are five phrases:

1) "Once upon a time..." (A sense of expectancy is needed here at the beginning of the story. The voice does not drop at the end of the phrase, but should suggest there is more to come.)

2) "...deep in the forests..." (A whole new thought is being expressed here. The setting of the story is being described and a feeling of mystery is suggested by the words. The first word of this phrase should be emphasized to distinguish it as important and different in quality from the previous word.)

3) "...of a distant land..." (Ah! Not only does this story take place in a mysterious forest, but it's set in a strange place as well! The sense of mystery is extended and the voice anticipates there is more to come).

4) "...there lived an old woman..." (Now we have a character in the story. As this phrase is a simple statement of fact, it should probably be read matter-of-factly.)

5) "...who was very lonely." (And now we know something about the character, perhaps something we can relate to, feel sympathy for, care about. The word "lonely" should be spoken in a way that suggests how loneliness feels. Etc.)

Have the student practice each phrase separately until it has the necessary feeling and meaning. Then have the student do several phrases together, and finally the whole sentence, getting feeling and meaning into each part. Record the last version. Play back the very first and very last recording and note the difference. Make sure the class can see this, too.

Teaching students to read and orally interpret phrases may be time-consuming at first, but once they catch on, you'll have to race to keep up with them--and you won't have to listen to any more monotone readings!

VOCAL PUNCTUATION
Punctuation marks are not merely used by writers to make their works easier to read. The various symbols of punctuation are used to express specific *feelings*. As such, they signal changes in vocal expression. Each mark infers its own feeling.

☺ *ACTIVITY: PUNCTUATION.* Write a sentence on the board. In round robin fashion, have each student choose a different punctuation mark to end the sentence, say what the punctuation mark means, and read it aloud until they're satisfied their reading conveys the correct meaning. (Have them try a period, comma, semi-colon, colon, dash, question mark, ellipsis... three dots... and exclamation point).

Approaching punctuation as clues to oral interpretation will help to more fully communicate the author's intention.

ATTITUDE
For every change in vocal nuance, there is a complementary change in emotional quality, or attitude.

☺ *ACTIVITY: ATTITUDE.* Pick five students, one for each of the following sentences. Have them say their sentence out loud.
1) "He was a mean, tight-fisted old miser."
2) "Sir, are you implying that I am guilty of deception?"
3) "Whenever she looked at him, her heart began to flutter wildly, her face felt flushed, and she seemed not to know what to do with her hands."
4) "The dreadful sound grew louder and louder, drawing closer at every moment."
5) "At long last, the sky was clear, a brilliant blue and crystalline in its clarity."

Notice how each of these sentences suggests a different attitude. Encourage your students to find and express the appropriate attitude for each phrase they speak. Have them all read aloud again.

FACIAL EXPRESSION ☺
It is really all right to look animated while speaking! It's difficult to read a tragedy intelligently while smiling. Or make sense out of a happy ending with a sour expression on your face.

☺ *ACTIVITY: FACIAL EXPRESSION.* In the activity above, have your students find a suitable facial expression for each attitude they express. Let them practice in front of a mirror, or see themselves on video so they can monitor themselves.

GESTURE
"Suit the action to the word, the word to the action," Shakespeare reminds us. The nodding or shaking of the head, a shrug of the shoulders, a clenched fist or a slouch in posture can not only enhance the verbal communication, but may also help the student become more involved in the emotional content of the words.

☺ *ACTIVITY: NON VERBAL ORAL INTERPRETATION.* Ask students to communicate a memorized speech without speaking any words, using only gestures to get all the nuances therein. This is not a game of charades: They are to use gestures to express the complete feeling and meaning of words, not to pantomime syllables therein. They should make the gestures as big and exaggerated as possible at first, using the entire body to communicate meaning and feeling.
Next, have them speak the speech aloud, keeping the same sized gestures they just used. Gradually, with repetition, the gestures will dwindle down to those essential to effectively communicate the meaning.

TEMPO
Neither too fast nor too slow is the usual standard for any recitation. But sometimes, the tempo may change even in the middle of a phrase.

☺ *ACTIVITY: TEMPO.* Have your students repeat aloud the sentences above, or others of your own choosing. First, very rapidly. Then, very slowly. Then fast on the first part and slow on the second. And vice-versa. Discuss which reading is more interesting and why.

RHYTHM

With "The Midnight Ride of Paul Revere," "Song of Hiawatha," many stories and poems from around the world, when read in their original languages, or most of Shakespeare (when read correctly), there is little problem with rhythm, because it's obvious. All published writers, however, journalists and novelists as well as poets and playwrights, not only select their words and syntax very carefully, but they also build in a definite rhythm to convey the subtext (underlying meaning) of their piece. Students need to experience lyricism, suspense, stateliness, and whatever other rhythmic qualities are contained in a literary piece, in order to appreciate the full flavor of the work.

☺ *ACTIVITY: RHYTHM.* Have your students discover the rhythms of their speeches through oral experimentation. And watch the delight in their eyes when they find it.

Yes, of course, it's important to read the words correctly and clearly and loudly enough to be heard. It is equally important that students understand and experience the meaning of what they read in order for them to truly go into, through, and beyond a piece of literature.

POINTING FOR EMPHASIS

Each sentence or clause (i.e., each complete thought) has a specific *point* to make.

☺ *ACTIVITY: POINTING A SPEECH.* Tell students to underline *one* word in each sentence they speak and emphasize that word by increase or decrease in volume, by a slight pause before and/or after the word, or in any other way that seems appropriate to the meaning of the words.

HOW TO READ A LINE

The above activity will greatly clarify the individual interpretation of any piece and help students to better understand what is written.

There is no "right" way to read a line. A line (or sentence or speech) should be read to express the author's intent through the actor's interpretation. It either communicates or it doesn't.

☺ *ACTIVITY: 'TWAS BRILLIG.* To have students recognize that *any* line may be spoken in a multitude of ways, have them try a round robin recitation of nonsense words, such as the first line of Lewis Carroll's "The Jabberwocky." Try for as many different interpretations as your students can come up with:

"Twas brillig and the slithy toves did gyre and gimble in the wabe."

(The record for a class of thirty students is 126 different interpretations.)

☺ **ACTIVITY: ORANGE JUICE.** This simple dialogue contains a wide variety of possible interpretations: a flirtation, an accusation, a threat, an invitation and so on. Have students, in pairs, work out their own version of it. See how many different interpretations you get:

"Orange juice?"
"No."
"Milk?"
"No."
"Coffee?"
"No."
"Tea?"
"No."
"Coke?"
"No."
"7-up?"
"No."
"Water?"
"Yes."

☺ **ACTIVITY: HAVE YOU SEEN MY PENCIL?** Follow the instructions given for the activity above ("Orange Juice"), but this time give each pair of actors a situation in which the following lines may be spoken. For example, two spies meeting in a park and speaking in code; a boy (and girl) trying to strike up a conversation; a distraught father trying to finish some paperwork and a child who has rocketed the pencil out the window; a magician who is searching for his magic pencil and an apprentice who has used the pencil to make herself invisible...etc.

Actor 1: Have you seen my pencil?
Actor 2: No, it isn't here.
Actor 1: Well, I left it here.
Actor 2: I haven't seen it.

☺ **ACTIVITY: A WALK IN THE GARDEN.** Follow the instructions given in the last two exercises. This time, however, give each student an individual motivation; for example, Actor 1 wants to murder Actor 2, while Actor 2 thinks he or she is being offered a job promotion; Actor 1 is secretly in love with Actor 2, while Actor 2 knows it and is not interested; Actor 1 has just won the lottery and wants to break the news privately to Actor 2, while Actor 2 has no money and is afraid Actor 1 is going to demand repayment of a loan; etc.

Actor 1: Would you like to take a walk in the garden?
Actor 2: Well, all right, if it doesn't take too long.
Actor 1: We'll be right back. Let's go.

After running through these exercises a few times, your students will be well aware of the variety possible in the oral interpretation of any prose, poetry, or dialogue.

☺   *ACTIVITY: PROJECTION AND ENERGY LEVELS.* Ask students to stand in a large circle. Choose a simple sentence. Tell them they are going to speak the sentence at ten different levels of volume, each level requiring a specific amount of energy:

> Level 1: Speaking to oneself so no one else can hear.
> Level 2: Speaking privately to the person next to them.
> Level 3: Speaking privately to the two or three people closest to them.
> Level 4: Speaking in hushed tones to the entire circle.
> Level 5: Speaking in normal volume.
> Level 6: Speaking loudly enough to be heard throughout the entire classroom.
> Level 7: Speaking loudly enough to be heard by a person standing just outside the open door of the classroom. (♪ *NOTE*: This level of volume is that used in most stage productions and TV sitcoms).
> Level 8: Speaking loudly enough to be heard by someone ten or fifteen feet away from the room.
> Level 9: Speaking loudly enough to be heard across the playground.
> Level 10: Projecting the voice to fill an imaginary football stadium.

Have students experience different levels, first from 1 to 10, and then switching back and forth at random to different levels. Monitor them closely. In a very short time, the students will know whether they are speaking at a 5, a 3, or a 7. And they will have a common reference point when you direct them to speak louder or softer.

Variation: Gesture Size. This same activity can also be used with size of gesture. With an advanced group, you might try having them gesture at a level 8, while speaking at a level 3, or gesturing at a level 4, while speaking at a level 9, and so forth. This exercise will greatly increase their versatility in both oral and physical interpretation. It will also help them to develop a common "stage language" by which they can monitor themselves and each other.

After all oral interpretation activities in this section have been done and the principles applied to the speeches students have been working on, have students record their speeches one more time. Tape this final version and play it back after playing the very first reading they ever did of the same speech. Note the improvement.

REHEARSALS

The best piece of advice ever given to actors preparing to rehearse:

"Speak the speech, I pray you, as I pronounced it to you, trippingly on the tongue: but if you mouth it, as many of your players do, I had as lief the town crier spoke my lines. Nor do not saw the air too much with your hand, thus; but use all gently: for in the very torrent, tempest, and, as I may say, the whirlwind of passion, you must acquire and beget a temperance that may give it smoothness. O, it offends me to the soul, to hear a robustious periwig-pated fellow tear a passion to tatters, to very rags, to split the ears of the groundlings, who, for the most part, are capable of nothing but inexplicable dumb shows and noise. I could have such a fellow whipped for o'erdoing Termagant; it out-herods Herod: pray you avoid it... Be not too tame neither, but let your own discretion be your tutor: suit the action to the word, the word to the action; with this special observance, that you o'erstep not the modesty of nature: for anything so overdone is from the purpose of playing. Whose end, both at the first and now, was and is, to hold, as 'twere, the mirror up to nature; to show virtue her own feature, scorn her own image, and the very age and body of the time his form and pressure. Now, this overdone or come tardy off, though it make the unskillful laugh, cannot but make the judicious grieve; the censure of the which one must, in your allowance, o'erweigh a whole theater of others. O, there be players that I have seen play,--and heard others praise, and that highly,--not to speak it profanely, that, neither having the accent of Christians, nor the gait of Christian, pagan, nor man, have so strutted and bellowed that I have thought some of nature's journeyman had made men and not made them well, they imitated humanity so abominably... And let those that play your clowns speak no more than is set down for them: for there be of them that will themselves laugh, to set on some quantity of barren spectators to laugh too; though, in the meantime, some necessary question of the play be then to be considered: that's villainous, and shows a most pitiful ambition in the fool that uses it. Go, make you ready."

William Shakespeare
Hamlet, III,ii

THE REHEARSAL PROCESS

Within the period between the conception of an idea and its execution lies the essence of the creative act.

Whether one is composing a symphony, preparing a meal, writing a book, painting a picture, or putting on a play, the process of selecting an idea and bringing it into tangible form to be shared with others is an exacting, inspiring, frustrating, and enlightening activity.

Self-knowledge, awareness of the needs and foibles of others, the principles of cooperation, individual and group responsibility, and the importance of listening and following directions are all educational objectives inherent in the presentation of any play for public performance. Should the content of a play contain one or more curriculum objectives (and virtually every play does, if it is carefully selected), then the entire rehearsal process becomes a complete creative educational system.

The traditional rehearsal period for a professional two-hour, non-musical production is approximately 120 hours. (The assumption in a professional production, of course, is that the players are already skilled performers and can devote their full time to preparation for performance.) Seldom, in an elementary school, will a performance be scheduled to run longer than 40-45 minutes.

Regardless of the length of the play, rehearsals may be roughly divided into four sections:

1) Read-thru and Blocking
2) Stage and Character Business
3) Run-thrus and Polishing
4) Tech and Dress Rehearsals

The following guidelines are based on the premise that the group is working with a script. For the rehearsal process involved in an improvisational piece, see *Improvisation*, p.30.

READING THE PLAY

Once casting has been set, it is usual to gather the players together to read the play aloud and discuss it. This is best done in one sitting and serves several important objectives:

1) For the actors, the playreading enables them to get a cohesive understanding of the story, the emotional content, characters *and* character relationships, the mood of each scene, and the basic themes developed throughout the script.

2) For the teacher-director, the playreading allows him or her to begin the process of visualizing the production needs and the specific interpretation of the script with the company which has been assembled. Strengths and weaknesses, personality relationships between cast members, and new possibilities for dramatic or comedic moments are revealed at this time.

Reading a script in its entirety for the first time can be an exhilarating experience for both actors and director. Any music to be used in the production, costume and set designs, models, photos from previous productions of the script, or other production plans available, may be used at this time to give the cast a better vision of what the performance will be like, to spark their imaginations, and give them a goal toward which to strive.

Certainly, misunderstood words and ideas will be explained. Character motivations may be discussed and, insofar as possible, the cast should leave the first reading with a clear understanding of the script and enthusiasm for the adventure upon which they are about to embark.

BLOCKING

Blocking is the establishment of character movements throughout the play. It is the most important visual element in the production, communicates character motivation more powerfully than any other element of production, and tells the story as effectively as the dialogue itself.

If, for example, two characters are facing each other center stage, having an argument, and one suddenly breaks away and crosses downstage right and sits in a chair, the visual movement suggests to the audience a change in the emotional content of the scene and prepares the way for new information to be communicated.

A written script is merely a skeletal structure. Even the richest imagination can only *begin* to envision what the final production will be like. Blocking starts "adding flesh" to the skeleton script and breathes life into the written words.

For student playwrights, seeing their ideas come alive for the first time on stage can be one of the most positive and exciting experiences of their lives.

Blocking should always be done in concert with the reading of lines from the script. The exact moment in the script when a character makes a particular movement will punctuate the dialogue and give it stronger meaning.

☺ *ACTIVITY: MOVEMENT TIMING.* To demonstrate this principle to students, have them say a line with a blocking movement *before* the line, *during* the line, and *after* the line. Have them notice how each one felt and what impression each made on those watching. This will help them develop a sense of timing, which in turn will give them more confidence in what they are doing and make your job a whole lot easier! Ask the audience members to make the same kind of evaluation.

It is best for the beginning director and actors to make sure all blocking movements are written down (See *Prompt Script*, p.105). The director's prompt script should have *all* the blocking written in an individual copy of the script. Use a pencil, for you will probably change your mind several times during rehearsals.

√ *TIP:* Most directors write out the blocking in their scripts for the entire play *before* the first rehearsal and then give the directions to the actors, scene by scene. This saves a lot of time and gives both directors and actors confidence during the beginning rehearsals. Pre-blocking, as it is called, may be made easier by having a scale drawing of the floor plan (p.123) or a model, and moving small objects representing actors from one place to another to create an interesting and meaningful visual pattern.

STAGE AREAS

Writing blocking directions is most efficiently done in a traditional "shorthand" or notation indicating in written form what the movements are to be.

The elements of this notation are based on some simple premises. First, the fifteen basic areas of the proscenium stage ("proscenium" refers to a traditional stage arrangement with the audience all on one side and the stage on the other; it differs from such other configurations as a thrust stage--audience on three sides--or staging in the round--audience on all four sides:

Areas marked *left* and *right* are always from the point of view of the actor facing the audience.

Stage areas are indicated by letter, rather than by words: For example, C=center; U=up; R=right; etc)

Upstage is away from the audience; downstage is toward the audience. (In the seventeenth and eighteenth centuries, when these principles were first developed, stages were raked, rising toward the back, so that when an actor was walking "upstage," he was actually walking *up* the slant.)

Each stage area has traditional psychological qualities, from the point of view of the audience:

C (center): the second strongest area on stage. Use it sparingly, so that when it *is* used, it may give emphasis to a scene.

DC (down center): the strongest area. Use even more sparingly.

UC (up center): strong, but considerably less so than the other center positions.

DR (down right): the third strongest area; gives the feeling of warmth and intimacy (probably because of our cultural tradition of reading from left to right. In Oriental theater, DL is more often used for important scenes than DR). Narrators are often placed DR. Love scenes are often played here.

R & UR (right and up right): good for entrances, doorways, etc.

DL (down left): seems to have a "conspiratorial" feeling. Good for plots, plans, discussions, etc.

UL (up left): considered to be the weakest area of the stage--least noticed by the audience. "Ghosts" used to traditionally enter up left.

Each of these may, of course, be varied by the placement of levels, stairways, entrances, etc. Play around with the use of areas. You'll find what best suits your own needs and preferences.

ACTOR POSITIONS

Actors' *positions* on stage also create different effects. The positions are:

Straight front	full back
1/4 (quarter) right	3/4 left
profile right	profile left
3/4 right	1/4 left

Straight front is so strong that it should be used only for important speeches or actions. Otherwise, its overall effectiveness is lessened.

Conversations between two actors should generally be staged in quarter positions; or in profile, if the players are engaged in intimate communication, or in conflict.

Three-quarter positions are usually weakest, but full back is nearly as strong as straight front.

BALANCE

For both visual and dramatic purposes, the director will usually want the stage to be balanced. Each scene is a series of *stage pictures*. The same principles of balance and composition apply to the stage as to a painting or photograph.

Balance may be achieved on stage by placement of scenic elements, by spatial relationships, or by the movement of actors.

Examples: (see also *Focus with Stage Picture*, p.25)

Balanced   *Unbalanced*

HELPFUL TERMS IN BLOCKING STAGE MOVEMENT

Upstaging	One actor standing or sitting upstage of another actor, forcing the latter to turn up stage (with back facing the audience) in order to speak to the former. This is to be avoided by both director and actors.
Blocking	Another use of the term. One actor standing in front of another actor, *blocking* them from the audience's view. Upstaging often blocks both the actor upstaged and the actor upstaging himself.
Countering	Making a compensatory movement when an actor crosses in front of you in order to balance the stage picture. For example, if you as an actor are standing on stage left with a group of other actors, and an actor crosses from stage right to join the group, it might be appropriate for you to *counter* a few steps to the right and focus on the new arrival.
Cheating	(The one time this practice is acceptable in school!) Adjusting the face and/or body to be better seen by the audience. The task of the director and actors is to create the illusion of reality, rather than to attempt to reproduce reality. Cheating sometimes enables the audience to view the scene as real, more so than if it were played completely naturally.
Scene Sharing	Opening the body positions so each actor in the scene has equal visual focus from the audience's perspective.

BLOCKING NOTATION

Symbols: X = cross
2 = to
R = right
DL = down left, etc.
⌢ = a cross *above* or behind another actor or set-piece.
⌣ = a cross *below* or in front of another actor or set-piece.
A = a capital letter may be used to designate another character (the first initial of their name).
Ⓑ = a capital letter circled may represent a set-piece or piece of furniture.

Thus: "Alonzo crosses down right behind the bed to Jose" may be written:

      A X DR⌢Ⓑ2 J.

Blocking should be written in the script next to the line of dialogue on which the movement is made. (See *Prompt Script,* p.105).

For complex movements of several characters simultaneously, a sketch of the floor plan may be useful. For example:

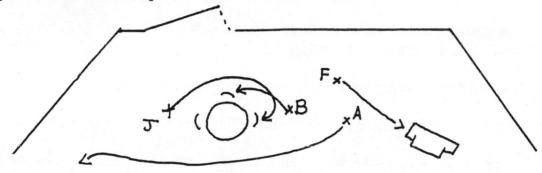

Translation: At the same time, Fernando crosses down left to armchair, Jose crosses above armchair to chair left of table, Benito crosses to chair upstage of table, and Alonzo crosses below table to down right.

It's a lot easier than it seems at first; and, after you've tried it a few times, you'll be noting your blocking like a pro! The students will enjoy it as well. To them, it's like learning a new and exclusive language. They'll catch on fast.

Blocking should be the first thing done after reading the play so that actors may learn their movements as they learn their lines.

It is best if the blocking is given scene by scene. The actors write down their moves for a scene and actually go through the notated movements. The scene should then be run again, so the blocking may be "set," i.e., established in the actors' minds to correspond to the dialogue. Then the next scene should be blocked and run, and so on until the entire show is roughly blocked. Care should be taken that the actors have written down their blocking correctly and that they go through their blocking as they learn their lines, in order that "the action may be suited to the words and the words to the actions..."

Once all the scenes have been blocked, then the entire play should be run to check that the actors know what they are doing and that there is a visual flow to the action.

TEN RULES FOR BLOCKING

I. Every movement must have three purposes: visual, psychological, and dramatic.

II. The direction of every move (horizontal, vertical, diagonal) is determined by: character, action, and the mood of the scene.

III. The shape of movements in a scene determines the quality of mood: e.g., long direct moves are dramatic; short, curved moves are comic; broad, sweeping moves connote grandeur; etc.

IV. The *timing* of movements determine the basic rhythm of a scene, thereby creating mood.

V. Movements illustrate emotional relationships.

VI. Blocking patterns determine basic set requirements (or vice versa). From the point of view of the director, the former is preferable.

VII. Blocking determines the essential visual composition of a scene.

VIII. Every movement means something to an audience.

IX. Movement in relationship to set pieces is determined by character and dramatic action.

X. Non-movement is as important as movement in establishing overall movement patterns.

A NOTE ABOUT LEARNING LINES

Seldom the grueling trial or amazing feat it is made out to be, learning lines is no more difficult than memorizing the multiplication tables or studying facts for a test. Indeed, like those activities, it is primarily a matter of discipline and (also like those activities) it is largely *homework*. Rehearsal time is too valuable, generally, to spend learning lines. The simplest technique, after roles have been assigned and the play has been read, is to silently read a sentence of a speech, look away from the script and repeat the sentence aloud. Then the next sentence. Then both sentences together, and so on.

Once the lines are roughly learned, then it is extremely helpful to have someone "cue" the actor; that is, read the sentence or phrase immediately before the actor speaks and then watch the script to check that the actor is memorizing the words correctly. This process should be repeated as often as necessary.

The person who is giving cues should simply read the words of the cue without attempting to emote. An interpretation other than the one the actor is used to is apt to be confusing.

After a certain period (ideally half-way through the rehearsal period and no more than two-thirds) all actors should have their lines "cold;" that is, thoroughly memorized. There is a limit to how much an actor can do on stage with script in hand. Give the actors as much help as you can, assigning others to cue them, or doing so yourself after school hours, if necessary.

If an actor forgets a line during rehearsals, there is no need for apologies or explanations. Simply calling "line" will suffice. Only the person holding the prompt script should give the actor the correct line. Other actors should refrain. Thus, it is wise to always have someone "on book" during rehearsals and even standing backstage during performances. Awkward as it may be, it is no sin to forget a line. Allowing that to break the actor's character or interrupt the flow of dramatic action, however, will harm the effectiveness of the scene.

✓ *TIP: A play is a series of emotional relationships*. If the actor knows the specific emotional quality to be conveyed through each line and memorizes the *emotions* in sequence, they will both learn the lines more easily and deliver them more effectively.

Blocking, business, and learning lines are the mechanical parts of the rehearsal process, the left-brained parts. Creating the characterizations and telling the story effectively are the right-brained, or creative parts. A successful performance is a blending of the two, so that the audience is aware only of the play and not the process that accomplished it.

WORK-THRUS

Work-thrus (blocking and business rehearsals) are rehearsals when you stop and start a scene again and again, in order to get specific moments of dialogue or movement as you want them.

RUN-THRUS

Run-thrus are those rehearsals during which you run the play in its entirety and give notes to the actors and/or crew afterwards. Every play should have several run-thrus before the first technical rehearsal.

✓ *TIP:* A "race-thru" may be helpful in the latter stages of rehearsal. This is a rehearsal in which nothing is left out--dialogue, blocking, business, even pauses--but which is run at top speed, as much as two or three times the normal rate. This is an excellent way to build actors' confidence in the picking up of cues (allowing no unplanned pauses between lines), to develop a sense of timing and rhythm, and to set a feeling of the entire play.

✓ *TIP:* Don't let your actors "anticipate." The action of a play should always convey the sense of happening for the first time as the audience is viewing it. Thus, actors must react to a line or bit of business *after* it happens, not before. This sometimes takes practice.

√ **TIP:** Take care that they don't "telescope" a scene; that is, do not let them leave out details of a piece of action which is crucial to the story or the timing of the whole scene. This happens more often in improvisation (p.32), but should be watched for carefully with any production. Only the director (and some accomplished actors) are aware of how long a scene should take. Any scene should take as long as it takes to get the details of the story across most effectively--no more, no less.

√ **TIP:** The word "focus," (see *Energy Focus*, p.25) if defined early and used throughout rehearsals, will become a signal to concentrate attention on the moment. It is extremely important during rehearsals that actors not on stage give their attention to whatever is happening there or leave the room. Actors playing a scene should not be distracted by other actors (or visitors). And the more energy those offstage give to the actors performing, the more energy the actors will be able to give to their performance.

√ **TIP:** "Places" is the signal that the scene is about to begin. That means actors are to prepare to enter, or get ready to perform and that everyone is to be quiet and focused on the stage.

√ **TIP:** "Curtain," in theater (whether or not an actual curtain is used), is the equivalent to a movie director's call for "action!" It means the scene should start. "Curtain" is also used to denote the end of a scene.

√ **TIP:** "Cut!" means to stop the action immediately.

STAGE BUSINESS

Stage business includes those actions necessary to tell the story of the play which are not covered by blocking: everything from packing a suitcase, to swordfights, to preparing and eating a meal on stage. Most of these actions will be indicated in the stage directions of any published script.

As soon as the blocking is finished and run, then actors should be given stage business so the play begins to take on enough details to make the story comprehensible to the viewer. The length of time to be taken on stage business will vary according to the complexity of the dramatic action. Certainly, it should be rehearsed in enough detail at this time to coordinate with dialogue and blocking.

For example, if an actor is packing a suitcase and moving around the stage to gather certain items to pack, *and* speaking lines of dialogue at the same time, it will be important to time the blocking and the business to fit the dialogue. For example,

Sam: I'm really looking forward to this trip! (*He reaches under the bed and pulls out a large, battered suitcase and, tossing it on the bed, begins taking clothes out of the nearby dresser and placing them neatly in the suitcase.*) Going to New York has been a dream of mine for years! (*cleaning out the top two dresser drawers*). Lucky I did some laundry yesterday! (*He looks around for a favorite sweater and spots it behind the chair down left. He retrieves it and folds it carefully and then lays it on top of the socks and underwear already in the suitcase*). One sweater ought to be enough this time of year. Ah, yes, shirts! (*He takes three or four crisply laundered and packaged shirts from the second dresser drawer and places them next to the sweater. He starts toward the closet down right, stops a moment, scratches his head and smiles, and then returns to the bed. He holds up the top shirt for Fred's perusal*). You know, my mother gave me this shirt. "For a special occasion," she said. I'd say this was a special occasion, wouldn't you? (*He laughs delightedly, replaces the shirt, patting it lovingly, and strides toward the closet*). I've got a new pair of slacks which will look just great with that...etc.

The combination of business, movement, and dialogue, when deftly handled, can create quite a convincing illusion of reality. Student actors often have difficulty, at first, speaking, moving, and performing actions simultaneously. Close attention to stage business will sharpen their thinking skills, help them to integrate words and actions, and give them a greater sense of involvement in the scene.

Handling props skillfully and realistically, while delivering lines, is an excellent way to quickly develop an actor's skills. Involving them physically will inevitably help them to overcome self-consciousness, simply because they will have so much to concentrate on, they will have less time to be nervous.

✓   *TIP:* Rehearsal props (substitutes for the actual production property, e.g., a paper cup for a goblet, a stick for a sword, etc.) should be used for rehearsal as soon as blocking is completed so actors will get used to having something to handle.

CHARACTER BUSINESS

Whereas stage business essentially tells the story visually, character business delineates the personalities involved in the story.

Character business is sometimes indicated in the stage directions, but is more often developed by the director or the actors themselves. If, for instance, in the preceding example, Sam is a nervous kind of fellow, usually haphazard in his behavior but containing himself because of the importance of his New York trip, he might be directed to dump the contents of the first two dresser drawers into the suitcase and *then,* thinking better of it, arrange them neatly. He might grab his favorite sweater, throw it in the suitcase, and fold it as an afterthought.

If on the other hand, he is a character who is compulsively neat, he may be overly careful in seeing that his socks and underwear are folded just so, and transfer them into the suitcase in the same order they were placed in the dresser drawers. He might wince when he notices the sweater has fallen behind the chair, inspect it for lint, moisten his finger on the tip of his tongue to get rid of a tiny spot on the sweater, and so forth.

Character business can add much richness to a scene--eating daintily or sloppily, glancing in a mirror periodically and patting one's coiffure, adjusting one's collar and cuffs, etc. Joan Blondell, while rehearsing for a dinner-theater production of "Come Back Little Sheba," developed a brilliant piece of character business. While fixing breakfast (an important piece of stage business), she was placing bacon in a skillet before frying it. Unable to immediately locate a dish towel to wipe the grease from her hands and, obviously unwilling to wipe her greasy hands on her bathrobe, she nonchalantly wiped them on her hair and continued preparing breakfast. That simple action communicated more about the character of Lola, which Miss Blondell was portraying, than might pages of dialogue.

The more such identifying bits of character business an actor can develop throughout the course of a play, the more believable the character is likely to be and the more interesting the play, both to the actors and the audience. (See *Characterization*, p.85).

SAMPLE SCRIPT PAGE

From "The Incredible Circus of Oz" by CES

GLINDA:
  WARN: *Sound #5*
  WARN: *Light #8*
  CUE: *Sound #5*
(Gesturing to the large book in the center of the room.) This is my magic book. In this book are recorded all the events which are taking place at every moment throughout the Land of Oz.

(She gestures again.) A thrill of harp music is heard and the pages of the large book turn slowly. The lights dim on GLINDA, the TIN MAN, the COWARDLY LION and the SCARECROW. Lights glow brightly in front of the book. A MOTHER, FATHER, and three CHILDREN enter, dressed in tattered, yellow clothing).
  CUE: *Light #8*

Shifting uncomfortably in chair.

LION: *(Seated ULC)* This is making me nervous.

Note: Tin Man seated L of Lion

SCARECROW: *(Seated R of Lion)* Shh! *finger to lips*

GLINDA: *(Seated R of Scarecrow)* Listen. *Raises hands for silence* — *Enter DR XC w/girl*

WINKIE MOTHER: We have to have food. The children won't grow if they don't eat properly.
  Enter DR X DRC w/boys

WINKIE FATHER: I'll go to the Wicked Witch's storehouse again today, and see if anything is left.
  XC ⌣ WF

TALL WINKIE BOY: I'll go around to all the neighbors and see if they have any food they can share.
  X2 R of TWB *Puts arm around brother's shoulders*

SMALL WINKIE BOY: I'll go with you. Maybe we can do some chores and get something to eat.
  X DLC

WINKIE MOTHER:
  WARN: *Sound #6*
  WARN: *Light #9*
Bimi and I will go into the woods and search for some berries which have been overlooked, or some wild vegetables growing hidden under the leaves.

(She wipes tears from the WINKIE GIRL's eyes and hugs her.)

WINKIE FATHER: *X2WM*   I'm glad the Wicked Witch is dead, but we served her for so long, we've forgotten how to work for ourselves.

WINKIE MOTHER: We'll learn again.

CUE: Light #9 _____

(The family embraces and exits in different directions. Lights fade from the center and come up again on the main characters). *WM xit DL; WF xit UL; TWB xit DR, SWB following.* all hug each other in turn.   *(Harp music sounds again)*

CUE: Sound #6 _____

THE PROMPT SCRIPT

The prompt script (or promptbook) may be the single most valuable tool a director uses in the course of a production.

Before rehearsals begin, it is used to write in pre-blocking, to make notes about characterization, begin lists of anticipated production needs, organize designs and floor plans, etc.

During rehearsals, the director, director's assistant or stage manager records script changes, new blocking, sound, light and stage cues, floor plans, and script interpretation in the prompt script.

During performances, the prompt script is kept backstage by the stage manager and functions as the "operating manual" for the running of the production.

After the performance, copies of the program, photos, and other relevant records of the production are included, the prompt script thus becoming a complete record of the production.

Many teacher-directors will file prompt scripts from past productions to be used as valuable references, should the same play be produced again at a later date.

MAKING A PROMPT SCRIPT

To make a prompt script, obtain a three-ring, loose-leaf binder and a package of loose-leaf paper, and enclose a copy of the script within it. There are two ways to do this. If the script is printed on both sides of the page, either 1) two copies of the script will be needed or 2) "windows" may be cut out of the notebook pages and the script pages attached inside the windows with cellophane tape. In any event, detach each page in turn from the script and tape it to a sheet of loose-leaf paper to be placed in the binder. It is frequently a good idea to have the script page taped to the right side page, as the binder lies open facing you. The left side will be blank and you will use it for writing on. Or be sure to leave large margins on all sides of the script for the writing of blocking, interpretation, etc.

✓   *TIP:* Use different colors for the notation of particular types of cues and warning signals, e.g., lights--red, sound--blue, scene changes--green, actor entrances--brown). These cues will, once finalized, be transferred to "cue sheets" by the stage manager and distributed to the respective "crew heads."

✓   *TIP:* As its name implies, the prompt script is used for prompting the actors on their lines. Only the director or whomever is holding the prompt script should ever prompt actors during rehearsals.

THE REHEARSAL PROCESS

When making up a rehearsal schedule, begin at the end and work toward the beginning. If you always keep the goal in mind, you will be more likely to adapt the time allotted to the best advantage for you and your actors.

Below is a sample rehearsal schedule of sixteen two-hour rehearsals for a forty-five minute play.

REHEARSAL SCHEDULE

Date	Day	Time	Rehearsal Process	Notes
			Read-thru	
			Blocking--Scene I	
			Blocking--Scene II	
			Blocking--Scene III	
			Blocking Run-Thru	
			Work-Thru:	Stage business
			Work-Thru:	Stage business
			Work-Thru:	Character business
			Run-Thru	Without Scripts!
			Run-Thru	
			Run-Thru	
			Dress Parade/Polish	Wear black shoes and socks
			First tech w/o actors	
			Second tech w/ actors	
			First Dress Rehearsal	
			Second/Final Dress Rehearsal	
			Performance	
			Performance	
			Performance	

CHAPTER SIX

BUILDING A PRODUCTION

"Each element has its own particular relation to the drama. And each element--the word, the actor, the costume--each has the exact significance of a note in a symphony. Each separate costume we create for a play must be exactly suited both to the character it helps to express and to the occasion it graces."

Robert Edmond Jones
"The Dramatic Imagination"

"IT'S MAGIC TIME!"

This chapter deals with creating an illusion for the audience, and with the necessity of using all the elements of creativity to do so.

Colored lights, the massive stone walls of a castle, the mysterious lushness of a forest, or the cozy warmth of a living room transport us to another time, another place. Characters clothed in silks or velvets, spangled tights or suits of armor stimulate our imaginations and help us to identify with personages larger and more exciting than we imagine our lives to be. The chirp of crickets, a fanfare of trumpets or the strains of ominous music stir our feelings and prepare us to become involved in what we are witnessing.

To begin with a stack of lumber, cans of paint, swatches of fabric, assorted wires and lighting instruments, and a collection of odds and ends which will become stage properties; and then to design, build, and set up a total stage illusion is one of the most creative, rewarding and educational experiences your students will ever have.

HOW TO INVOLVE STUDENTS WHO DON'T WANT TO PERFORM

All children can grow and become more self-confident by expressing themselves through creative drama. There are, however, some children who, for a variety of reasons, simply do not want to perform in front of an audience. Acute shyness, family religious convictions, or an honest distaste for the limelight may lead some students to--sometimes vigorously--decline the opportunity to appear on stage.

Whereas students should certainly be encouraged to perform, they should not be forced, nor in any way punished, for choosing to express themselves differently than their peers. And many creative opportunities exist for them in theater which do not require them to act. Research, scriptwriting, design and construction of production elements, and a variety of technical and administrative positions offer rich creative and educational opportunities.

When you and your students are first planning a production, you may want to make a list of non-performance tasks and ask for volunteers to execute them.

It is important to fully communicate to students that those who work behind the scenes are every bit as vital to having a successful production as are the actors. Carefully avoid any sense of competition or "class distinction" between the actors and the "techies." They are all members of the same team, working toward the same goal. It is vital they recognize and acknowledge each other's contributions.

Below are listed several production tasks which may give students the opportunity to participate in the creation of a production, without directly confronting an audience. Each of these tasks requires the assumption of individual responsibility and may be geared to an individual student's interests:

RESEARCH

You may be dramatizing an historical event. It will be valuable to have at least one student responsible to advise on historical accuracy, point out anachronisms, make suggestions on costume accessories, stage props, etc.

SCRIPTWRITING

One or more talented students overseeing the final draft of the script will add cohesion and style to your performance.

DESIGN

Even if the entire class develops the design of the show together, the finished production will look much better if there are student design coordinators who make sure colors don't clash, see that each total scene is aesthetically pleasing, oversee details of costuming (such as hairstyles, appropriate shoes and socks, use of personal jewelry, and costume repair), see that the set is properly decorated and that all properties look as they should, and so forth.

That this function is often overlooked is the reason so many school performances look less than attractive. There is no reason a student performance cannot be as pleasing to look at as it is enthusiastically performed!

CONSTRUCTION

The ability to work well with one's hands in sewing, cutting and pasting, or building, is as much a gift as is writing, designing, and acting. Sets, props, and costumes may have to be constructed, and the skills involved (including such things as eye-to-hand coordination, measuring skills, manual dexterity, arithmetical ratios, color mixing, and color coordination) offer opportunities for good, solid learning and accomplishment.

LIGHTING, SOUND, AND STAGE CREWS

Positioning and running lights on cue, selecting and or producing sound effects and music at appropriate times during a show, and changing props and set pieces between scenes all require critical thinking and organizational skills, cooperation, and coordination of one's actions with others.

Now for your perk! The more students you have assuming responsibility for the various aspects of production, the more time you will have to exercise your creativity in directing the play.

STAGE MANAGERS AND ASSISTANT DIRECTORS

It has often been stated that the two most important people in a production are the director and the stage manager. They are two entirely different functions, each requiring a different point of view.

Simply stated, the director's role is to attend to the creative, artistic, right-brain aspects of the production. The stage manager takes care of the practical, technical, left-brain aspects.

It is the stage manager who serves as liaison between the director and the technical personnel, who gets the cast together for rehearsals, sees to it rehearsal props are available when needed, checks cues for sound and lights during rehearsals and records them in the prompt script, makes lists of props and prop changes between scenes, checks the stage to make sure everything is in place before calling the actors to come on; and, during the show, remains backstage reading the prompt script and calling the cues (letting the technicians know what they are supposed to do and when). While it is the director's job to put the show together, it is the stage manager's job to see that each performance runs smoothly. This position is considered so important in the professional theater, the stage manager is the final authority backstage. Once the show is running, the director is not even allowed behind the curtain!

An assistant director is a blessing. Taking notes, rehearsing lines with actors, making sure you have paper and pencils, writing blocking in the prompt script, getting you coffee if you need it (yes, part of assistant directing is being a "gofer"), acting as a buffer for visitors in the middle of rehearsals, reminding you of when it's time for a break and any other kinds of assistance you need... These are tasks which make your job easier and provide excellent training for the student chosen as your assistant.

Many of the tasks listed above are sometimes assumed by the stage manager, but if you are fortunate enough to have enough people to do both jobs, have the stage manager concentrate on the technical requirements of the show and the assistant director focus on the creative process of putting the show together.

Ideally, your assistant director should know the show as well as you do and could, if necessary, get the production up on stage in concert with the stage manager, should you become unavailable at the last moment.

Rather than being positions of "busy work" or roles of less importance than those of actors, it may be that the assistant director and stage manager receive more comprehensive learning and a greater sense of achievement than anyone else involved in a theater production.

PRINCIPLES OF COSTUME DESIGN

The success of Renaissance Faires throughout the land over the past couple of decades is a testament to America's love affair with costumes. Everyone loves to "dress up." So much so, in fact, that "dressing up" is one of the first games children learn to play and (if the thousands of costume rental shops across the country are any indication) one of the last games they relinquish as they grow older.

The latest fashion fads in everything from sneakers to hair styles, designer jeans to earrings, is so important to many school children that "being in style" can seriously affect their self-esteem and social standing, while just as seriously affecting their parents' pocketbooks.

Costume design is so important the garment industry is among the wealthiest businesses in the world. Entire periods of history are most easily identified by powdered wigs, Gibson Girl sleeves, or flapper dresses. As architecture identifies place, so does costume identify time. Beau Brummel has earned a legitimate role in history (including plays, films, and volumes of biography) for doing absolutely nothing but designing costumes for himself.

Whether the socio-cultural moment gives birth to the design or the designer/artist creates history is both debatable and irrelevant. It is a simultaneous-immediate event.

In the late 1930's, *Gone With The Wind*, one of the most popular films of all time, was largely *about* costume and directly influenced the market for children's books for at least another two decades. Walter Plunkett's costume designs were specifically used as major plot devices throughout the film. Some of the most memorable moments in the movie are based on costume elements: the shoulder-exposing dress Scarlett so brazenly wears to the barbecue at Twelve Oaks; the scandal at the charity ball in Atlanta when Scarlett dances with Colonel Butler in her widow's weeds; the new hat Rhett brings back to Scarlett from Paris; the courtship that ensues from her decision, seen clearly in the mirror, to try the hat on backwards; the nightgown Melanie drops to drape over the "damn yankee" Scarlett has just killed, and her mother's earrings he dangles greedily just before she shoots him in righteous indignation; the dress Rhett forces Scarlett to wear of crimson velvet, feathers, and sequins which makes her look like the ante-bellum harlot she is, and which Melanie actually compliments as she welcomes Scarlett to show us what a good woman Melanie is; the dress Scarlett and Mammy whip up from a pair of curtains; the red taffeta petticoat Rhett presents to Mammy to finally win her friendship, and on and on and on.

At least three different books of paper dolls of *Gone With the Wind* characters were issued throughout the country for years after the film was released. (One set has recently been reissued by Ted Turner, who owns the movie rights.) About the same time, paper dolls and coloring books of popular film stars and their costumes began filling dime store emporium counters all over the United States. Simultaneously, good-looking teenage dolls with several changes of costume were just beginning to catch on. Thus began the fabulous "Barbie" empire and all the offshoots she and Ken produced (including Barbie's "militant nephew," G.I. Joe) who exist only to be endlessly robed and disrobed by millions of children.

The works of two costume designers, Leon Bakst and Erte, have been immortalized by having their designs shown at major exhibits in some of the most prestigious museums and galleries in the world.

The worldly preoccupation with the variety of ways people adorn themselves is not new. Queen Elizabeth I had, at one time or another, some twelve to fifteen hundred dresses in her wardrobe. Silk stockings were first created for her. She received black ones from France, as a gift. Elizabeth's father, King Henry VIII, is so identified with a particular style of costume that anyone who got reasonably good grades in history would instantly recognize an impersonator of Henry who was clothed in his traditional apparel.

Jesus' seamless garment, the robe so valuable as to be gambled over by the Roman soldiers who crucified Him, is generally seen as one of the sacred objects of veneration by traditional Christianity, along with the crown of thorns (another costume piece) and the cross.

Joseph's coat of many colors (his "technicolor dreamcoat") has become a spiritual-psychological metaphor of vast implications.

Costume design is used not only to identify periods in time, but also social or economic position within a period. The great religions of the world are easily recognized by the vestments (holy costumes) worn by their respective spiritual leaders. Paupers and kings, tradespeople of every sort, military personnel, pirates... every class in every society is recognized by its clothes. Even national differences are delineated by "national costumes."

In recent history, costumes have even been described as relating to a particular occupation, event, or time of day: "business suit," "house dress," "party clothes," "Sunday best," "evening clothes," "sportswear," are examples.

Contemporary mythic figures are known at least as much by their costumes as by their exploits: Darth Vader and Chewbacca, Superman, Batman, Wonder Woman, and the various comic-book superheroes, Count Dracula, Santa Claus, the funnel-hatted Tin Woodman, Dick Tracy's bright yellow hat and trench coat, and the checkered-gingham, red yarn wigs of Raggedy Ann and Andy. Even a national holiday, Halloween, is based on the wearing of costumes and is a multimillion-dollar-a-year business.

Costume design is the device by which mankind gives personality to the world. The way one sees oneself is the way one will dress. And thus, while it may be difficult to discover one's true nature by what one wears, certainly it is readily apparent what one thinks of oneself by what one puts on at home, at work, or at play.

Designing costumes is an enjoyable and creative pursuit. Not only do the designer/artists get to create a personality for each of the characters clothed, but they also learn much of history, culture, symbolism, and their own creative imaginations in the process.

There are, however, certain guidelines which can help designers to create the effect they want to achieve. These are the principles of color, line (or silhouette), fabric, trim, and accessories.

COLOR

Color is the optical effect of certain vibratory rates of light. These rays of light are prismatically transmuted from white or clear light. Color has a profound psychological effect on the human psyche. Through cultural symbolism in the race consciousness, color connotes specific emotional qualities and cultural activities. (For the traditional symbolic meanings of colors, see p.55).

COLOR COMBINATIONS

Color combinations have their own symbolic connotations in American culture; orange and black for Halloween; green and red for Christmas; red, white, and blue for U.S. patriotism and the 4th of July. Somewhat more subtly, pastel pinks, blues, yellows, and greens--the colors of spring flowers--suggest the season itself. The combination of red, orange, brown, and yellow suggests autumn. A combination of red, orange, and pink gives a Latin American feeling. The combination of scarlet and olive drab immediately conjures up images of the uniforms of the "Red" army. Black and white together indicate extreme formality (a "black tie affair" is the most formal of social occasions). Pink and blue are "baby" colors. Green, russet, and brown suggest the woods. Blue and green give the feeling of the sea.

Light, in its infinite varieties of manifestation, is what gives form to the world. Color is the means by which we discriminate between forms. In costume design, color is the simplest and strongest element with which designer-artists can create the precise quality of personality they wish to portray.

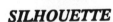

SILHOUETTE

In costuming, the outline of a garment is called the silhouette. Regardless of color, fabric, trim, or accessories, the silhouette powerfully conveys the sense of historical period. Learning to recognize the silhouette of various historical periods will help students to identify historical events both in terms of time and of space, and sometimes even of character. Notice the silhouettes illustrating this page for examples of this principle.

FABRIC

Most public schools have everything necessary to make costumes--except fabric. Butcher paper in the rainbow assortment of colors available can be used for hats, collars, cuffs, short tabards (a tabard is simply a rectangle with a hole in the middle for the head, useful for pages, musketeers, and even, with a little ingenuity and some scallops, a Robin Hood top), plumes, jewelry, fans, masks, some wigs, and various accessories. Laminated, the paper will even withstand several dress rehearsals and performances. For skirts, sleeves, capes, kimonos, breeches, harem costumes, and boot tops, however, there is no substitute for fabric. (Crepe paper can be near-miraculous in its versatility, but is often cost-prohibitive and difficult to find nowadays in the required quantities).

Do not despair, however. Your students' garages or attics and the friendly, neighborhood thrift store may offer a veritable infinitude of possibilities. Discarded negligees and nightgowns may be turned into gossamer gowns for princesses with a snip here and a tuck there. Skirts can be transformed into capes. Old blouses, velour bathrobes, lace curtains, window drapes, sheets, and even large swatches of fabric from neglected sewing projects are often available for only a few dollars and sometimes for free, if your students have understanding parents who haven't gotten around to delivering those cartons of discards to the Salvation Army.

The most important consideration for fabrics in costuming is their *draping* capability. Greek and Roman costumes, for example, *must* drape in soft folds to give any semblance of authenticity. Arabian Nights harem pants *must* be sheer. Elizabethan and Colonial skirts *must* be heavy enough to hold their shape. As for fabric design and color, use your own discretion, but read the section on color and color-combinations (above, p.113) and remember color *and* design make a definite statement. A terrycloth robe might be the basis for a Cowardly Lion costume, but not if it's a bright green plaid.

TRIM

Paper doilies, artificial flowers, bits of gold and silver paper, and pieces of costume jewelry can make the simplest costume appear magical on stage. A tabard of light blue paper may seem adequate; but add a dark blue strip of paper around the edges, a smaller white strip just inside the dark blue one, a *fleur de lis* of gold foil on a dark blue background in the center, complement it with a white shirt and a pair of black pants with blue ribbons tied around the knee, and you have a costume worthy of Prince Charming.

A pink leotard top over a pink blouse, with a pink bouffant skirt from an old formal may be the basis for Cinderella's ball gown, but add paper roses on the skirt and shoulders and some paper lace on the cuffs of the sleeves, pushed up to the elbow, and a round neckline, and you have a "fairy godmother creation."

ACCESSORIES

Paper fans; Navajo jewelry made from cardboard disks covered with aluminum foil, decorated with bits of colored paper and connected by strips of yarn; nineteenth century handbags made from gathered circles of fabric and decorated with paper tassels; Japanese parasols made from laminated circles of paper with painted designs, cut with a slit up the center and folded into the appropriate shape and attached to a pointer stick; a quiver made from laminated butcher paper and stuck full of sticks with paper-feather shafts protruding... These can make your costumes special, the actors proud of what they are wearing, and the audience entranced with the show. Yes, all these take more time, but it's time well spent if your students learn from the experience and have fun learning.

CHILDREN AS COSTUME DESIGNERS

If given a challenge, the ability to creatively express their imaginations, and guidance from you in the research and necessary skills, children love designing and building costumes almost as much as they love wearing them. Research, design, and construction of costumes provide rich learning experiences in every area of the curriculum. And after the performance, save the costumes for future use. Even display them along with the original designs. Your students will be as proud of their accomplishments in costuming as they will with a gold-star essay or an award-winning finger-painting. And you will experience a special glow of satisfaction as well.

ILLUSTRATION--PERIOD COSTUME SILHOUETTES

Ancient Egypt   Ancient Greece

Medieval Europe   Elizabethan England

115

ILLUSTRATION—PERIOD COSTUME SILHOUETTES

17th Century France

17th Century Japan

17th Century Iroquois

18th Century United States

19th Century United States

19th Century China

116

Masks are magical. Virtually every culture in the world has, at one time or another in its history, used masks for religious, shamanistic, theatrical or entertainment purposes.

The word "personality" comes from the Latin *persona*, meaning *mask*.

In each of us, there seems to be a kind of secret delight in disguising ourselves; in appearing to others as different, more mysterious, more beautiful, or more sinister than we consider ourselves to be in everyday life.

Children, with fewer socially imposed *personae* to mask their true natures, love both making masks and wearing them, whether from paper bags and construction paper, styrofoam plates, cups and balls, or life masks of plaster bandages painted to represent what they would like to be or what they fear they might be.

For educational purposes, masks may be used in numerous and interesting ways. Wearing a mask enables the student to move and act out feelings which might ordinarily be suppressed for fear of criticism by authority figures and/or peers.

Masks stimulate non-verbal communication, since neither facial expressions nor (in most cases) speech may be used to get across ideas and feelings.

Because the body (rather than the face and voice) becomes the main vehicle of communication, students gain a greater awareness of their bodies and the power of creative movement.

Artistically, movement with masks takes on a dimension of archetypal behavior and expands the students' versatility in creative expression.

ACTIVITY: MASK MAGIC. Allow students to experience the magic of masks by:
1) Selecting one of a variety of masks (constructed by students, recovered from Halloween or a party or play, etc.) and, after putting a mask on, trying different postures and movements in front of full-length mirrors.
2) Acting out a story in pantomime wearing masks, while the teacher narrates the story.
3) Passing a mask around a circle, each student donning the mask and doing a simple movement or gesture suggested to them by the mask itself.

NEUTRAL MASKS

A neutral mask is a simple, white full-face mask with eye-holes and a nose opening, but without any features painted on. Combining creative movement with neutral masks emphasizes the body language of kinetic movement: this is excellent for pantomime or movement to programme music (music which tells a story or sets a mood).

HALF-MASKS

Also known as "three-quarter masks," these masks (which may be made of any material) leave the mouth and jaw open so the actor can speak freely. Theatrically, these kinds of masks have a long tradition. They came into great popularity with the *comedia dell'arte* (improvisational troupes of professional actors who toured Italy and France in the sixteenth and seventeenth centuries, and from whence came the characters of Pantalone, Pierrot, Pierrette, Harlequin and Scaramouche).

In the late nineteenth century in Denmark, character half-masks came into popularity with

both children and adults alike. Many of the original designs have been reissued within the past couple of decades and may be purchased inexpensively at costume rental shops and some party supply stores.

Since the basic design of these masks is so simple, and so easily adapted to any character, the pattern is included here, along with examples of finished mask designs below. Providing students with a basic pattern and having them design their own masks based on characters either previously chosen or determined spontaneously, will enable them to design a recognizable character face for themselves and still exercise their creative imaginations.

☺ *ACTIVITY: MASK PREPARATION.* Place the mask you will wear on a table or desk in front of you. Make sure the area around the mask is cleared, so nothing distracts you from the mask itself. Study the mask. What does it make you think about? Put on the mask and look at yourself in the mirror for one full minute. How does it make you feel? Take the mask off and place it before you. Look at it again. Close your eyes and picture yourself playing the character represented by the mask. Put the mask on and react to everything around you as the character.

ILLUSTRATION: THREE-QUARTER MASKS

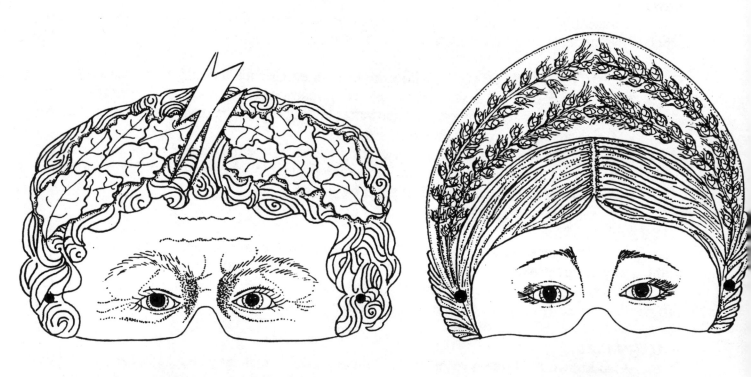

Zeus (Jupiter)   Demeter (Ceres)

118

BLANK MASK (3/4) REPRODUCIBLE

1. Add features, headdress, and color as desired.
2. Cut out and laminate Mas.

3. Cut out black spaces
4. Attach to head with yarn or string.

NOTE: Adjust space between eyes to child wearing mask.

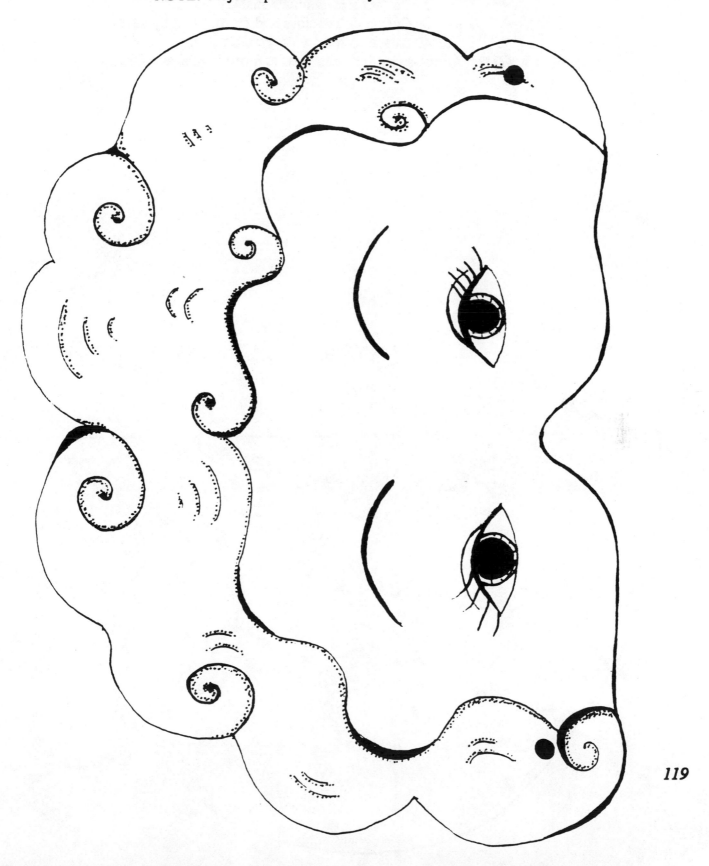

119

NEUTRAL MASK—REPRODUCIBLE

1. Add features, if desired.
2. Cut out and laminate mask.
3. Cut on dotted lines and cut out black spaces.
4. Attach to head with yarn or string.

♪ *NOTE:* Adjust space between eyes and/or mask size as necessary.

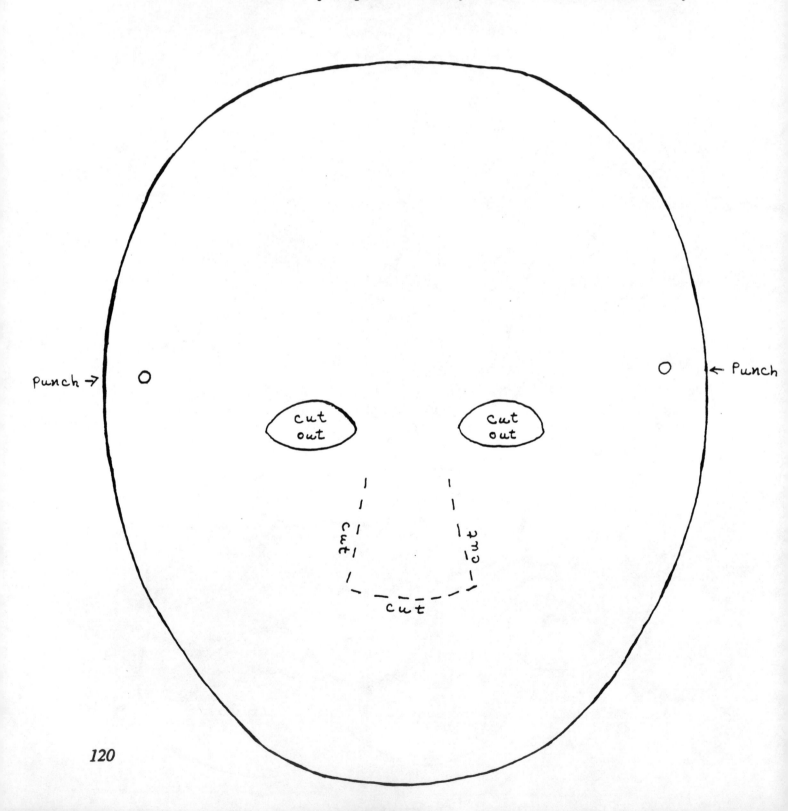

STAGE MAKEUP

Makeup is used on stage for three reasons: 1) to give color to the face, hands, and other exposed parts of the body under the intensity of stage lighting; 2) to highlight facial features, which are often "flattened" or "washed out" by bright light; and 3) to delineate characterization (old age, beards and mustaches, protruding noses and chins, animal features, etc.) Most classroom drama does not need makeup. Most productions on stage do.

✓ **TIP:** If you are using "base" makeup, use pancake or liquid, rather than grease. You'll find the cleanup significantly easier.

✓ **TIP:** Eyeliner, a little rouge (across the bridge of the nose as well as on the cheeks-- check your own skin color in the mirror, or that of a friend), and a light dusting with flesh colored powder is often all that is needed for most stage productions.

✓ **TIP:** Use water-based pancake for clown makeup. It's easier and neater to apply than grease, and may be removed with soap and water.

✓ **TIP:** Boys should almost *never* wear lip rouge, if you want them to look like boys. After applying base, lightly moisten a tissue and remove all makeup from the boy's lips. That should suffice to give a natural appearance.

✓ **TIP:** Makeup may be removed by cold cream and facial tissue. It may just as safely and effectively be removed by Crisco and toilet tissue.

✓ **TIP:** Help the girls in your class to understand that stage makeup is not necessarily for the purpose of making them look glamorous, but rather to make them look like the character they are playing (which in some cases may be an old hag).

♥ **BIG TIP:** Invite an artist-in-residence or a community theater actor to come to your class and teach the students to do their own makeup.

THE ELEMENTS OF SCENE DESIGN

Whether in a classroom, cafeteria, playground, or conventional theater space, scene design can be an effective part of the theater experience. Scene design provides focus for the dramatic action, identifies the locale, helps to create the mood of any scene, and indicates the theatrical style of the production.

Some will be familiar with the conventional "living room set" called for in many scripted plays (a sofa, a couple of chairs, a few tables, three or more doorways, perhaps a fireplace, possibly a window). Outdoor scenes are traditionally indicated by a painted backdrop, a tree and/or a bush (cut out and free standing), and often an overhead cut-out border of leaves stretching from one side of the stage to another.

Perhaps because these conventions are so deeply ingrained in our collective psyches as "the way a stage setting should look," many teachers despair of including scene design in their playmaking plans.

Consider alternatives:

A large American flag as a backdrop.

A large papier-mâché sun, mask, or crown upstage center against a blank wall or curtain.

Platforms arranged at various levels, perhaps with a chair, a bench, or a desk on each one to designate different locales.

Front screen or rear screen projections on a sheet with a carousel slide projector or from transparencies on an overhead projector.

A free-standing doorway with an ornate paper frame and a cut-out chandelier suspended from the ceiling to suggest a ballroom.

Colored cubes arranged like building blocks and changed into different patterns for different scenes.

Students making different shapes with their bodies (great fun and often very effective-- sometimes with the addition of masks or costume accessories, e.g., a clock face for a grandfather clock, strips of yellow, red, and orange crepe paper for a student playing the fire in a fireplace...)

The possibilities are infinite, limited only by the imaginations of you and your students.

Involve your students in the design process. It will develop their aesthetic perceptions, strengthen critical thinking skills, foster group cooperation, stimulate creative problem solving and stretch their imaginations. With the construction process, it will allow them to experience the practical application of measuring and motor skills, and give those students not comfortable with performing, the opportunity to become creatively involved with the project.

As with any other theater activity, the art of scene design is rich with educational potential.

HOW TO START: RESEARCH

Thorough familiarity with the story or historical event or concept is essential to begin any scene design.

Illustrations in storybooks are excellent resources for design ideas. You library has a wealth of visual material for perusal. So do magazines, film-strips, and videos.

The research for a design project can of itself be an educational enrichment. Consider the learning necessary to create a *fleur-de-lis* pattern on the drapery above a king's throne in a French fairy tale; the difference between the kinds of trees in the north woods, an African jungle, or a New England village; the different styles of architecture of a Greek temple, a Chinese pagoda, and an ante-bellum mansion; the kinds of fireplaces used in an Irish cottage, an Arthurian castle, or a suburban American home; the dwelling places of Plains Indians, the Pueblos, or the Aztecs, etc., etc.

DESIGN CONCEPT

When the first stages of research have been completed, the next step in scene design is to develop a *design concept*. This means determining how the scene will look. Realistic? Abstract? Like a particular book illustration? Satiric?... There is no right way or wrong way for it to look. It is purely a matter of creative choice.

But you have to decide. Are you going to set up one end of your room to look like a living room? Or are you going to drape bolts of fabric or crepe paper in great loops to make interesting shapes? Are you going to surround your audience with the action or will they enclose the playing space?

Once you settle on a design concept, you are ready to begin executing it.

FLOOR PLANS

After the imagination has been stimulated and the creative juices are flowing, it's time to become practical.

A floor plan is a bird's eye view of the stage or playing area, similar to a blueprint. You start with a floor plan in order to give your actors and yourself a guideline for movement. It then serves as a starting place for your scene designers.

A floor plan is necessary 1) to determine where furniture and set pieces will be placed for each scene; 2) to indicate to actors where they need to move during different points in action (after you have taught them how to read a floor plan, have them make copies of it and write down their stage directions for each scene) (see *Blocking*, p.95), and 3) to create a movement pattern for the play which is visually interesting, clear to the audience, and within which no one bumps into anyone else.

ILLUSTRATION - FLOOR PLAN

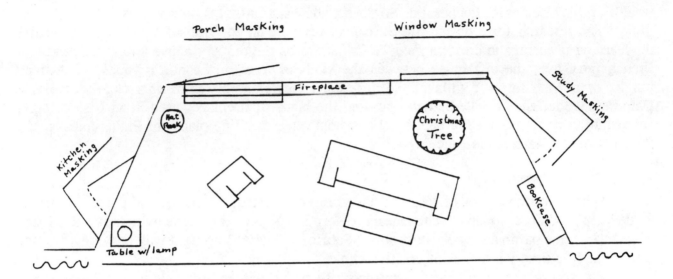

ILLUSTRATION - WORKING DRAWINGS

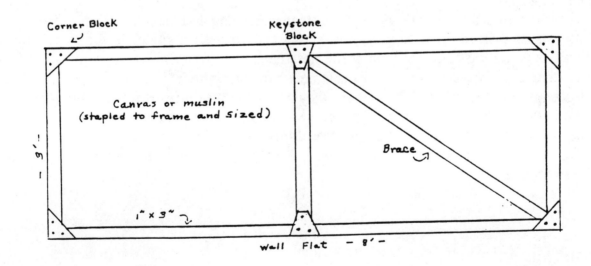

THE SKETCH

After you know where things will be on the stage, the next step is to determine how the playing area will be seen by the audience. At first, all you will need is a rough idea. So, after your designers have become familiar with the floor plan, have them sketch out a visual representation of each scene, following both the design concept and the floor plan.

This can be in pencil, charcoal, pastels, or crayon. It is for the purpose of combining both the conceptual aesthetic of the scene and the practical necessities (actors' movements, exits and entrances, placement of furniture, and so forth).

THE RENDERING

For those students who enjoy art, this may be their favorite step. It's now time to create a colored drawing of the scene (in any medium) as it will appear to the audience. Some basic sense of perspective may be helpful here, but it is not absolutely necessary. (There are several highly respected and very well paid scene designers who are incapable of rendering any but the most rudimentary perspective... so don't worry about it).

What is important in a rendering is color, ornamentation, and a relative sense of proportion.

Once a sketch for a scene has been selected, you may wish to make a line drawing of the scene yourself (or have a graphically-oriented friend do it for you) and have your students color it and add the appropriate ornamentation (fringe, lace or ruffles on draperies? Kinds of flowers growing? Shapes of clouds? Patterns of wallpaper?... etc.) Try having students render their interpretations of the selected sketch for the scene. Have the class decide which colors and/or ornamentation should be used. (See *Color*, p.55)

Make a final rendering to use as a visual reference.

WORKING DRAWINGS

For every piece of scenery that has to be built, it is extremely helpful to have a diagram of how it is to be built, with accompanying directions written next to the drawing. This enables the builders to know the exact dimensions of the piece, where to place nails or glue, and precisely how the piece is to be constructed. In addition to teaching students to follow directions, good working drawings are an aid to confidence and a sense of achievement when a piece is built as designed.

THE MODEL

A delightful project by itself for any student, the construction of a scaled cardboard model of a scene is a particularly appropriate project for gifted students, combining complex math skills in scaling down measurements, aesthetic perception through emphasis on three-dimensional replication, and manual dexterity in the construction of miniature pieces of cardboard and tape. Color sense is enhanced by the use of different pigments in painting the model, and by the effect of light and shadow on those pigments.

☺ *ACTIVITY: SET MODEL.* Construct a model set with your class. With paint, try several different colorings, and ask the class to discuss how each color choice affects the mood of the set. Then try lighting the set in different ways: from one side or another, brightly or dimly, with clear or colored light (flashlights with colored gels in a darkened room can be used for this purpose). Again, ask students to note the different moods created.

HOW TO FINISH

The final step in preparing your scene to be acted upon (once it is constructed, painted and ornamented) is *set decoration*. These are the final touches that give "reality" and individuality to a scene: books in the bookcase, andirons in front of a fireplace, a cushion on a throne, a scattering of leaves on the "ground" beneath a tree. It's like decorating a cake, or wearing jewelry. Set decoration makes the scene special.

And after your scene is decorated, you and your class can stand back and feel a sense of pride in having prepared a place for playmaking magic to happen.

BUILDING STAGE PROPERTIES

Medieval goblets can be made out of papier-maché, decorated with buttons and rope and sprayed with gold paint. Swords can be aluminum foil-wrapped cardboard. A sultan's throne can be an ordinary chair covered with a gaily painted butcher paper backing. Paper flowers can be used to create a garden, strips of cellophane on wire can become a fountain, and a painted crescent can be the moon.

With newspapers and coat hangers, cardboard and gold paint, metal foil and glue (items which can be found in any school or easily brought from home), virtually any kind of stage property can be constructed in the classroom.

Many normal crafts projects may be adapted to create "stained glass" panels, "tapestries," mosaics or miniature villages. The average elementary school teacher spends years teaching classes to make stage props, usually without being aware of it. This is where inspiration and imagination come in. Particularly if you are doing a play as part of a thematic unit, plan your crafts projects to serve double duty in constructing props or costume accessories.

Examples: Heraldic banners for the giant's castle in "Jack and the Beanstalk." Greek pottery for Mt. Olympus in the myth of "Demeter and Persephone." Tie-dyed or block printed T-shirts for an African folk play. A royal Egyptian necklace made from painted macaroni glued to heavy paper. Origami birds and ornaments for a Japanese fairy tale, etc.

Students usually enjoy making props as much as any other craft activity, and seeing their finished products on stage, being used as an important design component of a play, can enhance self-esteem and the sense of participatory involvement.

THE MAGIC OF LIGHTING

The biblical account of the creation indicates the very first element of the Creative Process was Light. Certainly, in our culture, light has become a metaphor for a number of our highest aspirations: wisdom, joy, awareness, understanding, grace. All visual and most performing arts depend on light for their existence. The color spectrum is the result of different wave lengths of light. Without light, we would probably be unable to survive in the world.

Sunlight and shadow, the glory of rainbows, the vibrancy of sunrises and sunsets, the varieties of candlelight, moonlight, torchlight, and artificial light in our everyday lives are so common that, while we may occasionally notice their beauty, we most often take the phenomenon of light for granted.

In our schools, light is almost exclusively considered in a purely functional way. As long as there is enough light to see by and not too much to be distracting, the quality of light in the classroom or cafeteria or office or auditorium is given little attention.

☺ *ACTIVITY: MOOD LIGHTING.* Change the mood of a class by lighting the room with table lamps with pink or soft white bulbs. Try a room flooded with amber light, or a room lit by candelabra. In each case ask students to describe the change in mood, in feeling.

Paper lanterns, Christmas tree lights, flashlights, or small, motorized color wheels, even strips of translucent colored paper hung over windows and light fixtures, may be used effectively either as part of a creative drama experience, or to enhance the study of a particular curriculum unit.

THEATRICAL LIGHTING

Theatrical lighting is generally used to create mood, e.g., red for passion or high tension; indicate time of day, e.g., blue for night; the passage of time, e.g., cross-fading slowly from white to pink to show the sun setting; special effects, e.g., a bright burst of white light to suggest an explosion; to change the audience's focus from one stage area to another (by fading lights in one area and bringing them up in the new one: *crossfading),* to begin or end a scene (fade up or out), and principally to make sure the actors are lit enough to be seen.

The stage lighting in many elementary school auditoriums (or stage areas in all-purpose rooms) is either inadequate for theatrical purposes, in a generally continual state of disrepair, or a mystery to most, if not all, of the staff.

Usually, the set-ups are easy to understand and simple to operate. And they are well worth the time it may take to become familiar with them, by virtue of the "magical" effects they can create.

TYPES OF LIGHTING EQUIPMENT

Some of the types of lighting instruments you may encounter in your school or in your exploration of lighting are described below. These include *ellipsoidals*, excellent instruments for focusing on a specific area on stage, and which come in many different sizes for smaller or larger auditoriums; *Fresnels*, which are boxy looking instruments, good for lighting less sharply defined areas; and *tungsten-halogen* (quartz) lights, usually reserved for special effects. These lights all produce "hot spots" (places on stage where the light is the brightest) and should be focused before the performance to make sure they are lighting the desired area.

☺   *ACTIVITY: FINDING THE HOT SPOT.* Turn on a single lighting instrument which has a "hot spot" focused on the center of the stage. Send actors on stage one at a time to look for and move their faces into the "hot spot" in order to have the most light on their faces. Once they can all accomplish this, turn on several instruments which are focused in different areas across the stage. Again, have actors come on stage individually, and walk across the stage, pausing in each "hot spot."

♪ *NOTE:* The above activity is not only helpful for actors to become accustomed to stage lighting, but also serves the purpose of making sure there are no "dark spots" across the playing area.

The above instruments are customarily suspended from metal pipes above the stage or, in some cases, over the heads of the audience; or they are clamped to lighting "trees," vertical metal pipes with horizontal branches, and anchored into heavy metal bases. These instruments usually have detachable gel frames at the front to hold colored gels in place (see *Gels*, below).

Scoops are flood lights within semi-sphere casings and are good for general washes of light (small scoops are available in hardware stores or large discount stores and are one of the cheapest, easiest instruments to get and use when improvising simple lighting). *Spot lights,* or follow spots, whereas they can be used for general illumination, are best used for putting someone in a tight pool of bright light, especially if they are going to move around, as in a music or dance number (if they are not moving, a tightly focused ellipsoidal or other stationary light will do).

If you cannot find the instruments listed above in your multi-purpose area, don't despair. Most school stages will have either *track lighting* or, in some of the older ones, *strip lighting*. The really old ones may even have strip *footlights*. (Footlights are seldom used in today's theater, except for musical comedy chorus lines or old-time melodramas, in which they can add an air of authenticity).

The strip lights will either have colored bulbs in them already, or be set up to be gelled in different colors (see *Gels*, below). Strip lights will provide a general wash on stage, but if they are wired properly, the green lights will all be on one circuit, the blues on another and the reds on still another. (Green, red, and blue are the primary colors in lighting). This allows you to get different color washes on stage by using them singly or in combinations. Strip lights are often used at the rear of the stage to light the backdrop, either placed on the floor and focused upwards or suspended from the stage ceiling and focused downwards. Track lights can sometimes be moved on their tracks and can give you some flexibility in focusing your light in specific areas.

Standard theatrical lighting systems have "dimmer boards." Each lighting instrument, or group of instruments, is wired to a "dimmer switch," which allows you to take that circuit from a complete "blackout" to brilliant light smoothly, at any rate of speed you choose. Depending on how you gel your instruments, you can also blend colors in almost an infinite number of combinations, creating sunrises and sunsets, crossfades between indoor and outdoor scenes, etc.

If your school has none of the above, and you are inspired to enhance your production with the magic of lighting, don't give up! Ask your school or district electrician to replace your all purpose room light switches with simple household dimmer switches. This will allow you to approximate a dimmer board. Purchase a few scoop lights at your local discount store. Cut gels to fit and attach them to the scoops with duct tape. Mount the lights (they usually come fitted with clamps) wherever you can (free standing volleyball or badminton net stands make wonderful lighting trees) and run heavy extension cords to the nearest available light socket. (Be sure to tape the cords to the floor with duct tape so that no one trips over them. And check out your lighting arrangement with the school custodian, too, to make sure it's safe). Assign the required number of students to operate each switch as necessary. Rehearse them well. And voilá! You're a magician.

✓   *TIP:* Make sure anyone working with lights remembers that instruments which have been on, even just a short time, will be HOT, and remembers to use all proper safety precautions when affixing lighting instruments with ladders or chairs.

GELS AND GOBOS

Gels (so called because they were originally made of gelatin, now manufactured from plastic) are easily obtainable colored transparent sheets which can create a wide variety of effects. Check the yellow pages of any large city under "Theatrical lighting," or "Lighting--theatrical supply." Also the ads in *Theater Crafts* or *Dramatics* magazines offer a variety of theatrical supply house catalogs. Locally, your high school theater or community playhouse may have gels or know of a nearby supply house.

✓   *TIP:* The general rule of thumb is that each playing area on the stage should be lit by two instruments, each placed at opposite sides of the stage at a 45° angle to the area lit. One of these instruments should be gelled with a warm color (flesh pink, bastard amber, straw, or salmon) and one with a cool color (usually daylight blue).

Gobos are cut-outs which, when placed in front of the lens of a lighting instrument, will project a pattern on the stage floor or on a backdrop.

LIGHTING CUES

The light changes in a play are referred to as the lighting *cues*. The more complex the lighting, the more imperative it is for the technician to *write down the cues*. This is a good idea for anyone on the running crew (those who operate some technical element during the performance such as lights, sound, and set changes).

Lighting cues for a performance are written down on *cue sheets*. This tells the lighting technician when to turn which lights on and off. A cue sheet should be clearly enough written that someone new could take over in an emergency and handle the lights. It should tell the technician what the cue number is (the precise order of the cue in sequence), when it happens (the word or visual action in the play), which circuits come on and which go off, and (if dimmer units are available) how long the cue takes to execute (some cues are so slow as to be imperceptible to the audience, as in a sunset, while some cues are instantaneous, e.g., a blackout).

Should a lighting technician be sitting in a position where it is impossible to see the stage (not the best of all possible worlds), cues will have to be relayed from the stage manager via hand signals or headset.

Generally, at least one or two students in any class will be interested in lighting. Help them to explore the equipment available, guide them toward the appropriate reading materials (see *Bibliography*, p.139), and perhaps ask a friend or parent to share their expertise. The interested students will appreciate and learn from it, and your production will be thereby enhanced to a surprising degree.

Remember, lighting plays a very important role in the attraction of rock concerts, movies, television productions, shopping malls, and Nature itself. Your stage performances (and your classroom lessons) can be equally attractive by using the same principles and techniques.

LIGHTING CUE SHEET

LIGHTING SHEET FOR "Incredible Circus of Oz"						
Cue #	Page	Dimmers involved	End Reading	Cue to start	Time length of cue	Notes
#8	107	6 7 8 11 15	3 10	Harp thrill "	5 seconds "	
#9	107	15 6 7 8 11	0 8½	Family Embraces	10 seconds	
#10	108	22 23	Bump to 10 then fade to 0	Glinda: "I hope they're safe!"	1 seconds 4 seconds	"Explosion" effect.

SOUND AND MUSIC

Sound is a powerful stimulus in creating mood and suggesting a specific environment. Students respond enthusiastically to the inclusion of sound and music in both classroom drama and stage productions.

Theater is an excellent vehicle through which to introduce types of music which may not ordinarily interest many students. Recorded classical programme music (music that is meant to depict or suggest a particular scene or story, or mood) can be quite effective before, after, under, or between scenes. A selected list of programme music is included in Appendix D. Ethnic music can also be extremely potent in evoking an unfamiliar culture.

Orf instruments or other rhythm instruments played by students may provide excitement in a play for both performers and audiences.

Sound effects records (or tapes) are not difficult to obtain (check your local theatrical supply house or community theater) and can create an environment of sound with traffic noises, foghorns, animal sounds, wind and rain, or birdsong.

Last to be usually considered, but certainly not least in enjoyable learning, are radio sound effects which the students themselves can build and operate: wind and rain machines, sheets of aluminum shaken to make the sound of thunder, cellophane crumpled in front of a microphone to give the effect of a crackling fire, etc. Check out some of the books on technical theater listed in the bibliography, call a local radio station for advice, or arrange a field trip for your students to visit a recording studio.

One or more of your students may become fascinated with the world of sound and become your sound technician(s) for the year.

Listening for the appropriate cues, executing a sound effect at the right time and at the correct volume takes practice, but can be a major factor in making your overall production memorable for everyone involved.

TECH AND DRESS REHEARSALS

A technical rehearsal is one which is devoted to the integration of sound, lighting, props, scene changes, and special effects into the production. Often, the first "tech" rehearsal is held without actors, in order for the production crew to practice timing, volume and brightness levels, and to be as exact in their contribution to the production as are the actors. Obviously, they will have practiced on their own under your direction or that of the stage manager and/or assistant director. The first technical rehearsal is their opportunity to translate theory into function.

Everyone needs a lot of patience at a tech rehearsal (which is why actors are often omitted at the first one). A music cue may have to be run again and again to get the timing and volume levels as desired. Lights may have to be repositioned. A first tech rehearsal for even a simple production may take hours.

The second tech rehearsal usually includes actors and is usually run "cue-to cue." That means that an actor will give the cue for a sound or lighting effect (See *Prompt Script,* p.104). The effect will be run in its entirety, the actor will continue as the cue which ends the effect passes, and then the director or stage manager will cut to the next technical cue, and so on until all the cues are run correctly.

Actors often find tech rehearsals somewhat disconcerting. They are, by this time, so engrossed in playing their roles, that the introduction of new elements into the play may seem almost an intrusion. Don't be overly concerned about this. They'll get used to it. And most of them will be aware enough to realize all these new elements will serve to make the play--and their performances--even better. If they don't realize this on their own, tell them!

Expect your first dress rehearsal to be somewhat chaotic. They usually are. Actors will have to deal with sound, music and light for the first time at a full rehearsal. They will be wearing different costumes than their normal dress for the first time and are liable to be uncomfortable, skittish, confused, incredibly awkward, and distracted. They are likely to forget things and make seemingly incomprehensible blunders. Costume pieces may be too large or too small. Pins may still be in some of them and jab the actors in uncomfortable places. Colors may clash, an actress may discover she can't sit down in a hoop skirt, pieces of business may have to be changed as a result, an actor may miss an entrance because he cannot figure out the mystery of hooks and eyes. In retrospect, it will all seem hilarious, so take a few deep breaths and plunge ahead--you're almost home! This is, after all, the first time everything has come together in one place. Adjustments are to be expected.

✓   *TIP:* A *dress parade* will help somewhat to ease the confusion of the first dress rehearsal. This is a rehearsal solely for the purpose of all the actors trying on their costumes (as completely as possible) and showing how they look--individually and in relationship to one another--to the director. Ideally, this is the time to do refitting, make changes, and practice stage movements in costume. A dress parade should be scheduled two or three days before the first dress rehearsal in order to give the costumer(s) time to make any necessary changes.

There is a long-standing tradition in theater that "a bad dress rehearsal means a good performance." This maxim may have been invented by an optimistic or a desperate director. The fact remains, however, it is often quite true. "Why" is a matter of endless speculation, but it's probably simply a matter of working the kinks out, combined with the rush of adrenalin symptomatic of opening performances.

It is most helpful to have a small audience at the final dress rehearsal--another class, friends, loyal parents, crew members, etc. Actors need at least one chance to get used to people laughing, or applauding, or otherwise reacting to their performances before confronting an opening.

After the final dress rehearsal, the best advice for both actors and directors is, "Get plenty of rest and get here in plenty of time to be ready to open." A "call" is generally set for a time at which everyone is expected to be there (for students at least an hour ahead of performance is desirable).

THE PERFORMANCE... AND AFTER

Not many experiences are more thrilling than the opening of a play. The air fairly crackles with excitement. Weeks of preparation are about to culminate in a performance which will be fresh and new for the audience and which will allow actors, designers and technicians to present their finished work for the first time. Anticipation runs high.

Before every performance, actors should be in costume and makeup at least one half-hour before curtain time. Lighting and sound levels should be checked. Props to be brought onstage by actors should be checked by both the stage manager and the actors who use them. The stage set-up should be checked by the stage manager according to his notes in the prompt script.

Actors should be encouraged to conserve their energy for performance and not indulge in unnecessary chatter and horseplay.

After the half-hour call is given by the stage manager (the announcement that curtain time is half an hour away), no one should be allowed backstage except those directly involved in the performance.

The stage manager should also give calls for "10 minutes," "5 minutes," and "places." At "places," all technicians are to be at their posts and all actors are prepared to enter on cue.

Five or ten minutes before "places" is called, it is helpful for the director to call the cast together for last-minute instructions, the calming of nervous tension, and a few words of sincere encouragement.

√   *TIP*: During your pre-performance "pep-talk" remind your actors of the following:
1. Once the "house is open," and the audience has begun to assemble, the theatrical experience has begun, whether or not the actors have come on stage yet. Therefore, cast and crew must be aware that anything they do will affect the audience's enjoyment of the show. They should avoid such things as peeking through the curtain, or appearing in a visible part of the playing area to set props or get something (unless this is a pre-planned part of the event). The same rule applies during intermissions. Actors should never appear before the audience in costume and makeup until after the performance is over.
2. If a cue is missed (either a technical cue or a line forgotten by an actor), improvise. Remember, the audience doesn't know what is supposed to happen. They will accept whatever they see and hear as the way it's supposed to be, unless an actor lets them know, by body language, breaking character, or facial expression that something has gone wrong.
3. Stay in character. No matter what happens, react to it as your character, rather

than as yourself. If a piece of scenery falls down, ad-lib a comment about poor construction of the building. If an actor fails to appear on cue, improvise some dialogue about the character never being on time for anything, and if possible, get one of the actors to go off stage to look for the missing truant. If a telephone rings when it shouldn't, answer it, listen for a moment, and tell them they have the wrong number. Whatever happens, make up something, anything, to stay in character.

4. Have fun. If you're having a good time, so will your audience. That's why you're on stage, to be in a "play."

Directors will find it advisable to take notes during performance (for cast *and* crew) and to either give the notes after the show or, with ample time for assimilation, before the next performance.

POST MORTEM

After the production has closed (the condition of the facility, the rehearsal and construction spaces, and everyone's lives restored to normal), it is useful to hold a "post-mortem," during which a discussion is held to evaluate the production with all those who were involved. Not only will this crystallize the experience for both you and your students, it will also help everyone to do a better job next time!

"We believe every American should have quality opportunities to be educated in all the arts. Such an education should occur both in and out of schools as part of each person's total learning process. All individuals, including those with special talents or needs, learn not only from arts education experiences provided by arts specialists, but also from classroom teachers, professional artists and community resources. Only by utilizing all these existing arts resources can all individuals achieve the full educational potential of the arts."

Education Program
John F. Kennedy Center
for the Performing Arts

134

CHAPTER SEVEN
EXPANDING YOUR HORIZONS

"You have not done enough, you have never done enough, so long as it is possible that you have something of value to contribute."

Dag Hammarskold

Theater is a communal experience. This chapter is about using all the resources your school and community have to offer.

No man is an island. And no teacher is alone. If there is agreement on anything in the world today, it is the universal recognition of the ever-increasing need for better education for all young people.

Even though there may be disagreements as to teaching and administrative methods, curriculum content, and the socio-economic status of teachers, everyone looks forward to the next generation being smarter, more self-confident, more compassionate, and better prepared to deal with life than is the present generation.

Teachers are looked upon as a team these days, each responsible for one another, and all responsible for every child in the school. Education is a more popular subject in the media, politics, and business than ever before. Parents are being encouraged to become involved in their children's education. Teacher support groups, associations, and organizations abound.

You need help? Just ask. Do you have a spouse who can type, or who has recording equipment, or who can sew? A friend who has an old box of forgotten costumes or Halloween masks in the attic or garage? A colleague who has an extensive record or tape collection, or who studied drama in college, or who plays a musical instrument? A student's parent who is talented in art, or carpentry, or electrical wiring?

Involve them! Most people, if approached with respect and friendliness, will gladly share their time and talents for the benefit of children.

Pledge to make every arts-in-education experience for your students as celebrative and enlightening as humanly possible. Ask for whatever help you need. Involve as many people as you can. The children will love the attention. Your friends, colleagues, and students' parents will love the opportunity to share. And your school will love the community involvement. As for you, you will have the experience of having created a learning situation in which everyone benefited. And your own ability as a teacher and your self-esteem will grow thereby.

"We are part of the Whole and will receive our own needs from any holistic action... There is no them, there is only us!"

WTS

UNEXPLORED RESOURCES IN YOUR OWN SCHOOL

When is the last time you really looked into those dusty cardboard boxes stored over or under the stage in your school auditorium, or in the janitor's closet, or in the physical education office, or in last year's "lost and found"?

How much do you know about the non-clerical skills and interests of your office staff? The maintenance staff? The food service staff? Abolish labels of people by function and see them as the wonderfully whole, fascinating, unique individuals they are.

Have you really perused all the material in your Resource Room? Old 78rpm records which might be transferred to tape and used as musical background for a show? Outdated textbooks or magazines which just might contain an activity, poem, or technique which could propel you to new heights of learning or teaching? An old game which, if revised and spruced up with a little paint, could be just the thing your students need to grasp a concept, learn a skill, or develop an ability?

Most schools which have been around for a few years, are an unexplored storehouse of the care, concern, and creativity of past students, teachers, and administrators. And it is often true that priceless treasures may be found among the discarded or forgotten.

Go on a scavenger hunt. Better still, organize one with your students (after establishing necessary ground rules and obtaining requisite permission, of course). Children are able to see their world with fresher eyes than we can ours, and just may teach you that your very own school is a more wondrous place than you ever imagined.

UNEXPLORED RESOURCES IN YOUR COMMUNITY

There is probably enough cardboard thrown away in a week from the retail stores in your community to provide stage settings for every production in every school in the area for over a year. Restaurant supply houses sell lacy paper goods at a fraction of their price anywhere else. Fabric stores almost inevitably have bins of slightly damaged fabric which they are happy to get rid of. Lumber companies store large containers of scrap materials which they are often willing to donate, as do upholstery shops, construction sites, and film production studios. Clothing stores sometimes discard clothes which have been faded by the sun in showroom windows, or which have been inadvertently soiled. Jewelry manufacturers often throw away cartons of unused or out-of-date beads and fittings.

Thrift stores usually have embossed brass platters, artificial flowers, large swatches of fabric, packages of yarn, tea sets and cooking utensils, table lamps and second-hand sheets (sized with diluted white glue, these are an excellent substitute for canvas or muslin on flats), tablecloths, old books, costume jewelry, stuffed animals, and literally tons of clothes, many of which can be used as costumes (old formals and dressing gowns can often be adapted to provide "royal raiment" or cut up for their lace trim, satin bows, and netting). And most of these items may be found very inexpensively.

Does your town or city have a community theater? Or a window display house? A quilt-making guild? Crafts store? Party supply house? Travel agency? All can provide useful sources for donated or borrowed items.

Do your local museums and libraries have educational programs? Do nearby consulates provide educational materials about their countries? Does your local college or university have graduate students who might be willing to share what they are learning? Is there a doll-collecting club near you? Toy stores and children's book stores might jump at the chance to display their wares for your students and share their knowledge at the same time.

What about celebrities? Gregory Peck, John Lithgow, and John Ritter are among the movie stars who have visited schools simply because some teacher thought to write and ask them. Is there a local architect who loves kids and would like to talk to them? A noted musician? Or historian? A cable TV company which is interested in educational programming?

Does your local arts council offer artist-in-residence programs? Does your chamber of commerce sponsor programs for children? Are there members of local service clubs who might be persuaded to take part in school activities?

Without question, a school is an invaluable resource to any community. It is, indeed, the hub of a community's growth and progress. The community is also a resource for a school, and one of vast potential. It needs only to be tapped.

Love is not only the feeling,
Love is the action.
The feeling is that of existence.
The quality of one's existence
Depends on the quality of one's love.
Love is the action.
"You" is the feeling.
So feel Good—
Love!

WTS

APPENDIX A: BIBLIOGRAPHY

CHAPTER I:

Bernardi, Bonnie, and others. *Partners in the Arts: An Arts-in-Education Handbook*. New York: American Council for the Arts, 1983.

Broudy, Harry S. *The Role of Imagery in Learning*. Los Angeles: The Getty Center for Education and the Arts, 1987.

Coming to Our Senses: The Significance of the Arts for American Education. New York: American Council for the Arts, 1978.

Fowler, Charles. *Can We Rescue the Arts for American Children? Coming to Our Senses Ten Years Later*. New York: American Council for the Arts, 1988.

Gardner, Howard. *Frames of Mind: The Theory of Multiple Intelligences*. New York: Basic Books, Inc., 1983.

Gardner, Howard. *Art, Mind, and Brain*. New York: Basic Books, 1982.

Katz, Jonathan, ed. *Arts and Education Handbook*. New York: American Council on the Arts, 1987.

McLaughlin, John, ed. *A Guide to National and State Arts Education Services*. New York: American Council on the Arts, 1987.

McLaughlin, John, ed. *Toward a New Era in Arts Education: The Interlocken Symposium*. New York: American Council for the Arts, 1988.

Steiner, Rudolf, and others. *Education as an Art*. Blauvelt, NY: Steinerbooks, 1981.

"Toward Civilization: A Report on Arts Education." Washington, D.C.: National Endowment for the Arts.

CHAPTER II:

Avital, Samuel. *Mime and Beyond: The Silent Outcry*. Studio City, CA: Players Press, 1990.

Avital, Samuel. *Mime Workbook*. Studio City, CA: Players Press, 1990.

Berdard, Roger L. *Dramatic Literature for Children: A Century in Review*, Anchorage, KY: Anchorage Press, 1983.

Belt, Linda and Rebecca Stockley. *Improvisation Through Theatre Sports*. Seattle: Thespis Productions, 1989.

Fast, Julius. *Body Language*. New York: Lippincott, 1982.

McCaslin, Nellie. *Creative Drama in the Classroom*. fifth ed. Studio City, CA. Players Press, USA, 1991.

McCaslin, Nellie. *Creative Drama in the Primary Grades*. Studio City, CA. Players Press, USA, 1987.

McCaslin, Nellie. *Creative Drama in the Intermediate Grades*. Studio City, CA. Players Press, USA, 1987.

O'Neill, Cecily and Alan Lambert. *Drama Structures: A Basic Handbook for Teachers*. Portsmouth, NH: Heinemann Educational Books, 1982.

Poulter, Christine. *Playing the Game*. Studio City, CA: Players Press, 1991.

Rowlins, George and Jillian Rich. *Look, Listen and Trust*. Studio City, CA: Players Press, 1992.

Salisbury, Barbara T. *Theatre Arts in the Elementary Classroom*. New Orleans: Anchorage Press, 1986.

Spolin, Viola. *Improvisation for the Theatre: A Handbook of Teaching and Directing Techniques*. Evanston, IL: Northwestern University Press, 1983.

Spolin, Viola. *Theatre Games for the Classroom: A Teacher's Handbook*. Evanston, IL: Northwestern University Press, 1986.

Way, Brian. *Development Through Drama*. Atlantic Highlands, NJ: Humanities Press, 1973.

Way, Brian. *Audience Participation: Theatre for Young People*. Boston: Walter H. Baker Company, 1981.

CHAPTER III:

Heathcote, Dorothy. *Collected Writings on Education and Drama*. Evanston, IL, Northwestern University Press, 1991.

Siks, Geraldine B. *Drama with Children*, second ed. New York: Harper and Row Publishers, Inc., 1983.

Stewig, John Warren. *Informal Drama in the Elementary Language Arts Program*. New York: Teachers College, Columbia University, 1983.

Wagner, Betty Jane. *Dorothy Heathcote: Drama as a Learning Medium*. Washington, D.C.: National Education Association, 1976.

Wagner, Jearnine, and Kitty Baker. *A Place for Ideas - Our Theatre*. San Antonio, TX: Principia Press, Trinity University, 1977.

CHAPTER IV:

Bressven, Carol Ann and others. *Wouldn't It Be Wonderful: An Integrated Curriculum to Meet Student Needs for the 21st Century: Self Esteem, Global Awareness, Conflict Resolution, Children and Fear*. Educational Extension, University of California: Riverside, CA, 1989.

CHAPTER V:

Asher, Sandy. *Where Do You Get Your Ideas? Helping Young Writers Begin*. New York: Walker and Company, 1987.

Barton, Arthur. *The Director's Voice: Twenty-One Interviews*. New York: Theatre Communications Group, 1990.

Boleslavsky, Richard. *Acting: The First Six Lessons*. New York: Theatre Arts Books, 1975.

Brook, Peter. *The Empty Space*. New York: Atheneum, 1978.

Cassaday, Marsh. *Playwriting Step-By-Step*. San Jose, CA: Resource Publications, 1984.

Catron, Louis E. *The Director's Vision: Play Direction from Analysis to Production*. Mountain View, California: Mayfield Publishing Company, 1989.

Cole, Toby and Helen Chinoy. *Directors on Directing*. Indianapolis: Bobbs-Merrill, 1963.

Dean, Alexander and L. Karra. *The Fundamentals of Play Directing*, fifth ed., New York: Holt, Rinehart, & Winston, 1989.

Egri, Lajos. *The Art of Dramatic Writing: Its Basis in the Creative Interpretation of Human Motives*. New York: Simon and Schuster, 1972.

Joucla, Peter. *Absurd, Black and Comic Sketches*. Studio City, CA. Players Press, USA, 1991.

Needlands, Jonothan. *Structuring Drama Workshop: A Handbook of Available Forms in Theatre and Drama*. Cambridge, NY: Cambridge University Press, 1990.

Ommanney, Katherine Anne and Harry H. Schanker. *The Stage and the School*, fifth ed. New York: McGraw-Hill, 1982.

Roddy, Ruth Mae. *Monologues for Kids*. Toluca Lake, California: Dramaline Publications, 1991.

Sawyer-Young, Kat. *Contemporary Scenes for Contemporary Kids*. Boston: Baker's Plays, 1986.

Self, David. *The Drama and Theatre Arts Course Book*. Studio City, CA. Players Press, USA, 1992.

Stanislavsky, Constantin. *An Actor Prepares*. Trans. by Elizabeth Reynolds Hapgood. New York: Theatre Arts Books, 1989.

Williams, Guy. *Choosing and Staging a Play*. Studio City, CA: Players Press, 1990.

CHAPTER VI:

Allensworth, Carl, with Dorothy Allensworth and Clayton Rawson. *The Complete Play Production Handbook*, rev. ed. New York: Harper and Row Publishers, 1982.

Asher, Jane. *Jane Asher's Costume Book*. Menlo Park, California: Open Chain Publishing, Inc., 1991.

Barton, Lucy. *Historic Costume for the Stage*, renewal ed. Boston: Walter H. Baker Co., 1963.

Belleville, Cheryl Walsh. *Theatre Magic: Behind the Scenes at a Children's Theater*. Minneapolis: Carolrohda Books, Inc., 1986.

Burris-Meyer, Harold and Edward Cole. *Scenery for the Theatre*, second ed. Boston: Little, Brown, 1972.

Corey, Irene. *The Mask of Reality: An Approach to Design for the Theatre*. Anchorage, KY: Anchorage Press, 1968.

Corey, Irene. *The Face is a Canvas*. New Orleans: Anchorage Press, 1990.

Corson, Richard. *Stage Makeup*, eighth ed. Englewood Cliffs, NJ: Prentice-Hall, 1981.

Fuchs, Theodore. *Stage Lighting*. New York: Ben Bloom, 1963.

Govier, Jacquie. *Create Your Own Stage Props*. Englewood Cliffs, NJ: Prentice-Hall, Inc., 1984

Gruver, Ben. Revised by Frank Hamilton. *The Stage Manager's Handbook*. New York: The Drama Book Shop, 1972.

Holkeboer, Katherine Strand. *Patterns for Theatrical Costumes: Garments, Trims and Accessories from Ancient Egypt to 1915*. Englewood Cliffs, NJ: Prentice-Hall, 1984.

Holkeboer, Katherine Strand. *Costume Construction*. Englewood Cliffs, New Jersey: Prentice-Hall, 1989.

Hunnisett, Jean. *Period Costumes for Stage and Screen* (2 volumes, 1500-1800 and 1900-1909). Studio City, CA. Players Press, USA, 1991.

Ingham, Rosemary and Elizabeth Covey. *The Costumer's Handbook: How to Make All Kinds of Costumes*. Englewood Cliffs, NJ: Prentice-Hall, 1980.

James, Thurston. *The Theater Props Handbook*. Whitehall, VA: Betterway Publications, Inc., 1987.

James, Thurston. *The Prop Builder's Molding and Casting Handbook*. Whitehall, VA: Betterway Publications, Inc., 1989.

James, Thurston. *The Prop Builder's Mask-Making Handbook*. Whitehall, VA: Betterway Publications, Inc., 1990.

Jans, Martin. *Stage Make-up Techniques,* second ed. Studio City, CA: Players Press, USA, 1992.

Jones, Robert Edmond. *The Dramatic Imagination*. New York: Theatre Arts, 1956.

Kelly, Thomas A. *The Back Stage Guide to Stage Management*. New York: Back Stage Books, 1991.

Parker, W. Oren and Harvey K. Smith. *Scene Design and Stage Lighting*, sixth ed. New York: Holt, Rinehart & Winston, 1990.

Williamson, Walter. *Behind the Scenes: The Unseen People Who Make Theater Work*. New York: Walker and Company, 1987.

CHAPTER VII.

Balfe, Judith H., and Joni Cherbo Heine, eds. *Arts Education Beyond the Classroom*. New York: American Council on the Arts, 1987.

APPENDIX B: STORIES TO DRAMATIZE IN THE CLASSROOM

Each of these stories which are commonly taught in the elementary grades offer a wealth of possibilities for integrated curriculum study, are easy to dramatize, and are fun for children to act out.

K-2
Baboushka and the Three Kings
The Blind Men and the Elephant
Coyote and the Moon
The Elves and the Shoemaker
The Gingerbread Man
Goldilocks and the Three Bears
How Coyote Stole Fire
The Little Engine That Could
The Little Red Hen
Little Red Riding Hood
Lon Po Po
The Magic Orange Tree
Nursery Rhymes
Stone Soup
Strega Nona
The Tale of Peter Rabbit
Three Billy Goats Gruff
Where the Wild Things Are
Why Mosquitos Buzz in People's
        Ears

3-4
Aesop's Fables
All Stories Are Anansi's
The Banza
The Bremen Town Musicians
The Children's Blue Bird
Cinderella
East of the Sun and
        West of the Moon
The Frog Prince
Hansel and Gretel
Indian Cinderella
It Could Always Be Worse
Jack and the Beanstalk
Knee High Man
Mufaro's Beautiful Daughters
Peter and the Wolf
Red Slippers
Rumpelstiltskin
The Princess and the Pea
The Selfish Giant
Sleeping Beauty
The Tongue Cut Sparrow
The Ugly Duckling
The Velveteen Rabbit
Winnie the Pooh
Yeh-Shen: A Cinderella Story

5-6
Amahl and the Night Visitors
Charlotte's Web
Crane Wife
Doctor Doolittle
The Emperor's New CLothes
The Fire Bird
The Hobbit
Johnny Appleseed
Johnny Tremaine
King Arthur and the
        Knights of the Round Table
King Midas and the Golden Touch
Legend of the Bluebonnet
The Lion, the Witch and the Wardrobe
The Little Prince
Little Women
Mary Poppins
Momotaro, the Peach Boy
Pandora's Box
Pinocchio
The Prince and the Pauper
Robin Hood
Sky God's Daughter
The Three Musketeers
The Tiger, the Brahmin and the Jackal
Tom Sawyer
Uncle Bonqui and Godfather Malice
Why the Chimes Rang
The Wind in the Willows
The Wise Men of Chelm
The Wise Old Woman

and any myth, legend, folktale, or fairy tale

APPENDIX C: PLAYS FOR CHILDREN

For reading copies of the plays listed below, contact Players Press, P.O. Box 1132, Studio City, CA, 91614. (818) 789-4980.

These plays require royalty payments for public performances. (This usually means that they are better written than plays listed as "non-royalty").

J.M. Barrie	*Peter Pan*
Jesse Beers, Jr	*Beauty and the Beast*
Robert Bolt	*The Thwarting of Baron Bolligrew*
Mary Chase	*Mrs. McThing*
Elizabeth B. Doolittle	*Aladdin and the Wonderful Lamp*
Olive Evans	*Secrets of the Forest*
Olga Fricker	*Hugh Lofting's Doctor Doolittle*
Richard George (adaptor)	*Charlie and the Chocolate Factory*
William Gibson	*Rag Dolly* (musical)
Jules Eckert Goodman	*Treasure Island*
Elizabeth F. Goodspeed	*The Wizard of Oz*
Nicholas Stuart Gray	*Beauty and the Beast*
	The Hunter and the Henwife
	The Imperial Nightingale
	The Marvelous Story of Puss In Boots
	New Clothes for the Emperor
	The Tinderbox
Ernie Guderjahn	*A Children's Trilogy*
Pat Hale	*The Ballad of Robin Hood*
	The Bremen Town Musicians
Aurand Harris	*Androcles and the Lion*
	Circus in the Wind
	The Flying Prince
	Pinocchio and the Indians
Raymond Hill	*Treasure Island*
Glenn Hughes	*The Magic Apple*
William Alan Landes	*(Wondrawhoppers)*
	Aladdin 'n his Magic Lamp
	Alice 'n Wonderland
	Grandpa's Bedtime Story
	Jack 'n the Beanstalk
	Rapunzel 'n the Witch
	Rumplestiltskin
	Rhyme Tyme
	The Wizard of Oz
Maurice Maeterlinck	*The Children's Blue Bird*
Lillian & Robert Masters	*Barnaby*
	Hansel and Gretel
	The Mystery of the Ming Tree

Darwin Reid Payne	*The Canterville Ghost*
Barbara Robinson	*The Best Christmas Pageant Ever*
Hansjorg Schneider	*Robinson and Friday*
Way, Brian	*Pinocchio*
Jessie Braham White	*Snow White and the Seven Dwarfs*
Gary Williams	*The Burning Fiery Furnace*
	David and Goliath
	Moby Dick
Gifford W. Wingate	*The Lion Who Wouldn't*

COLLECTIONS OF PLAYS FOR CHILDREN

Bradley, Alfred and Michael Bond. *Paddington on Stage*. Boston: Houghton Mifflin, 1977.

Donahue, John Clarke. *The Cookie Jar and Other Plays*. Minneapolis: University of Minneapolis Press, 1975.

Donahue, John Clarke and Linda Walsh Jenkins, ed. *Five Plays from the Children's Theatre Company of Minneapolis*. Minneapolis: University of Minnesota Press, 1975.

Doolittle, Joyce, ed. *Playhouse: Six Fantasy Plays for Children*. Ontario, Canada. Red Deer College Press, 1989.

Harris, Aurand. *Six Plays for Children*. Austin, Texas: University of Texas Press, 1977.

Howard, Vernon. *Complete Book of Children's Theatre*. Garden City, NY: Doubleday, 1969.

Jarvis, Sally Melcher. *Fried Onions and Marshmallows and Other Little Plays for Little People*. New York: Parent's Magazine Press, 1968.

Jennings, Coleman A. and Aurand Harris, ed. *Plays Children Love*. New York: Doubleday, 1981.

Jennings, Coleman A. and Gretta Berghammer, ed. *Theatre for Youth: Twelve Plays With Mature Themes*. Austin, Texas: University of Texas Press, 1986.

Kammerman, Sylvia E., ed. *Dramatized Folktales of the World*. Boston: Plays, Inc., 1971.

Lifton, Betty Jean, ed. *Contemporary Children's Theatre*. New York: Avon Books, 1974.

Mamet, David. *Three Children's Plays: The Poet and the Rent, The Frog Prince, The Revenge of the Space Pandas or Binky Rudich and the Two-Speed Clock*. New York: Grove Press, 1986.

Olfson, Lewy, ed. *Classics Adapted for Acting and Reading*. Boston: Plays, Inc., 1965.

Winther, Barbara. *Plays from Folktales of Africa and Asia*. Boston: Plays, Inc., 1976.

PUBLISHERS OF PLAYS FOR CHILDREN
Write and ask for a catalog!

Anchorage Press
P.O. Box 8067
New Orleans, LA 70182

Baker's Plays
100 Chauncy Street
Boston, MA 02111

The Dramatic Publishing Company, Inc. 311
Washington Street
Woodstock, IL 60098

Players Press, Inc.
P.O. Box 267
Kippax, A. C. T. 2615
AUSTRALIA

Players Press, (UK)
20 Park Drive, Romford
Essex RMI 4LH UK

Players Press, Inc.
P.O. Box 1132
Studio City, CA 91614 USA

Samuel French, Inc.
7623 Sunset Boulevard
Hollywood, CA 90046
or
25 West 45th Street
New York, NY 10036

APPENDIX D: MUSIC

A SELECTED LIST OF MUSICAL COMPOSITIONS FOR BACKGROUND MUSIC

This is necessarily only a partial list of some of our favorites. The possibilities are virtually endless. And what a wonderful way to introduce youngsters to the finest music in the world! Music, of course, is a powerful medium of communication. It will create mood, stir emotions, and underline the theme of any scene. In addition to the composers listed below, many fine composers (especially those of the late nineteenth and early 20th centuries) who are less well known than those whom we consider the "greats," have produced marvelous compositions which might be perfect for classroom drama or full-scale productions. Explore ethnic music as well. And the many fine musical scores from films. A classroom filled with music can be a classroom filled with joy.

Anderson	"Sleigh Ride," "The Syncopated Clock"
Beethoven	"Symphonies 3, 5, 6, & 9"
Berlioz	"Symphonie Fantastique"
Bizet	Orchestral selections from "Carmen"
Borodin	"Steppes of Central Asia" & "Polovtsian Dances"
Debussy	"La Mer," prelude to "L'Après-midi d'un Faune" & "Golliwog's Cakewalk"
Dukas	"Sorcerer's Apprentice"
Grieg	"Peer Gynt Suite" & "Norwegian Dance"
Herbert	Orchestral selections from "Babes in Toyland"
Holst	"The Planets" Suite
Lizst	"Liebestraume"
Mendelssohn	"Overture to A Midsummer Night's Dream" & "Italian Symphony"
Mozart	"Eine Kleine Nacht Musik"

Mussorgsky	"Night on Bald Mountain" & "Pictures at an Exhibition"
Offenbach	"Tales of Hoffman" (orchestral) & can-can from "Orpheus in the Underworld"
Prokofiev	"Classical Symphony" and "Peter and the Wolf"
Ravel	"Mother Goose Suite"
Respighi	"Fountains of Rome" & "Pines of Rome"
Rimsky-Korsakov	"Scheherazade"
Rossini	"William Tell Overture"
Saint-Saens	"Carnival of Animals" & "Danse Macabre"
Strauss, Johann	Waltzes, Polkas, etc.
Strauss, Richard	"Thus Spake Zarathrustra" & "Dance of the Seven Veils" from "Salome"
Stravinsky	"Rite of Spring," "Firebird Suite," & "Petroushka"
Tchaikovsky	"The Nutcracker," "Sleeping Beauty," "Swan Lake," & "Romeo and Juliet"
Verdi	Triumphal march from "Aida"
Vivaldi	"The Four Seasons"

APPENDIX E: ARTS-IN-EDUCATION RESOURCES

Alliance for Arts Education
Education Office
Kennedy Center for Performing Arts
Washington, D.C. 20566
202-416-8847

Amer. Alliance for Theatre and Eductn. (AATE)
Theatre Arts Department
Arizona State University
Tempe, AZ 85287
602-965-7788

American Theatre Arts for Youth
1429 Walnut Street
Philadelphia, PA 19102
215-563-3501

Arts in Education Program
National Endowment
for the Arts (NEA)
1100 Pennsylvania Avenue NW
Washington, DC 20506
202-682-5426

California Alliance
for Arts Education (CAAE)
State of California
Department of Education
P.O. Box 94472
Sacramento, CA 94244-2720

The California Arts Project
Glenda Gentry, Director
c/o Marin County
Office of Education
P.O. Box 4925
San Rafael, CA 94913
415-499-5896

Classroom Drama (newsletter)
Maynard Thomas Publishing
P.O. Box 14753
Orlando, FL 32857-4753
305-658-1539

Consortium for Pacific Arts and Cultures
2141C Atherton Road
Honolulu, HI 96822
808-946-7381

East Central Theatre Conference (ECTC)
Jerome O. Hanson, President
Box 428
Gettysburg College
Gettysburg, PA 17325
717-337-6061

The Getty Center for Education in the Arts
1875 Century Park East
Suite 2300
Los Angeles, CA 90067-2561

Mid-America Arts Alliance
912 Baltimore Avenue
Suite 700
Kansas City, MO 64105
816-421-1388

Mid-Atlantic Arts Foundation
11 East Chase Street
Suite 2-A
Baltimore, MD 21202
301-539-6659

National Arts Education Association
1916 Association Drive
Reston, VA 22091
703-860-8000

National Assembly of Local Arts Agencies
(NALAA)
1420 K Street N.W., Ste. 204
Washington, DC 20005
202-347-6352

National Endowment
for the Humanities
1100 Pennsylvania Avenue
Room 503
Washington, DC 20506
202-786-0310

New England Foundation for the Arts
678 Massachusetts Avenue
Cambridge, MA 02139
617-492-2914

New England Theatre Conference (NETC)
50 Exchange Street
Waltham, MS 02154
(617) 893-3120

South East Theatre Conference (SETC)
506 Stirling Street, UNC-G
Greensboro, NC 27412
(919) 272-3645

Southern Arts Federation
1293 Peachtree Street N.E.
Suite 500
Atlanta, GA 30309

Theatre Communications Group, Inc.
355 Lexington Avenue
New York, NY 10017
212-697-5230

Western States Arts Federation
236 Montezuma Avenue
Santa Fe, NM 87501
505-988-1166

The Winifred Ward Memorial Fund
c/o Muriel Mawer
1201 Third Avenue
Suite 2900
Seattle, WA 98101

GLOSSARY

A

actor - one who acts (either male or female).

actor coaching - helping an actor with characterization, line readings, appropriate movement, etc.

actress - a female actor.

ad lib - to insert improvised dialogue into a scripted performance.

anticipate - to react before the cue is given.

arts-in-education - hyphenated by the authors to indicate a specific, integrated, arts-oriented approach to curriculum study.

B

backdrop - a floor to ceiling piece of scenery at the rear of the stage.

base makeup - usually a flesh-toned makeup applied to the actor's face.

blackout - a sudden extinguishing of all stage lights.

blocking - movements of actors from one place to another on stage.

blocking - one actor standing in front of another hiding the latter from view of the audience.

bump - to suddenly raise or lower light or sound levels.

business - activities by actors during the course of the scene.

C

call - an announcement of time given to actors and crew prior to starting a rehearsal or performance. E.g., a call of "half-hour" means one half hour until the start of the performance.

cast - actors chosen to perform a play.

casting - choosing which actors will play which roles in a play.

character analysis - the detailed study of the idiosyncrasies of a particular character.

cheating - turning the face or body slightly towards the audience in order to gain fuller visibility.

counter movement - movement by an actor for the purpose of balancing spatial relationships after another actor has made a move.

creative drama - dramatic activity which depends largely on games, exercises, and improvisation.

creative dramatics - creative drama as a discipline.

crew - those responsible for the construction and or operation of a technical element in a play (e.g., lights, sets, sound).

cross - a movement on stage from one place to another.

crossfade - in lighting, to simultaneously fade out one circuit of lights while fading in another; in sound, to simultaneously fade out one sound or musical piece while fading in another.

cue - the words or actions immediately preceding an actor's speech.

cueing - reading the cues in sequence to an actor while he or she recites the lines from memory.

cue sheet - a written outline indicating when various technical effects occur during the course of a play.

curtain - a direction given to actors used either to begin or to end a scene.

D

dialogue - speeches between characters in a play.

dimmer - a fader switch or rheostat which allows gradual increase or reduction in light level on a given circuit.

dimmer board - the control center of any theatrical lighting system: the group of dimmers which control all lighting circuits in the theater.

director - the person who coordinates all the elements of a production into an artistic whole.

downstage - the area of the stage closest to the audience.

dress parade - a gathering of actors in full costume before final rehearsals.

dress rehearsal - a final rehearsal with all technical elements in place.

dramatization - the adaptation of any material into dramatic form.

E

exposition - dialogue in a script which explains the existing situation.

F

fade - to increase or decrease sound or light levels gradually.

fade in - to gradually increase the level of sound or light.

fade out - to gradually decrease the level of sound or light.

fade up - same as "fade in."

flat - a rectangular piece of stage scenery, traditionally constructed of a wooden frame and canvas or muslin covering.

floor plan - a "bird's-eye" view diagram of a stage setting.

focus - a direction given to actors indicating the need to concentrate intensely on what is happening at the moment.

focus - the center of visual attention of a scene.

G

gel - a sheet of colored plastic affixed before the lamp of a lighting instrument to give color to the light.

gel frame - metal frame attached to the front of a lighting instrument into which can be placed a selected colored gel.

gesture - a hand or arm movement.

gobo - a silhouette design placed in front of a lighting instrument to cast a shadow pattern on a backdrop or on a stage floor.

gofer - an assistant who "goes for" coffee, takes messages, etc.

I

image - a mental picture.

improv - short form of "improvise" or "improvisation."

improvise - to compose and/or perform on the spur of the moment without preparation.

integrated curriculum - a curriculum in which disparate elements are brought together to form a comprehensible whole.

in-the-round - a kind of staging in which the audience is seated on all four sides of the playing area.

L

light tree - vertical metal pipe with branching horizontal arms on it, anchored to a portable, heavy base, which serves as a place to attach stage lighting instruments.

line - a character's speech in a script.

line - the drape, shape, or silhouette of a costume.

M

mime - acting without words, or one who acts without words.

O

objective - that which the character in a scene is trying to achieve.

P

pantomime - acting without words or (usually) without using real objects.

part - the character (or role) assigned to an actor.

"pick it up!" - a direction given to actors urging them to accelerate the pace of the scene.

picking up cues - delivering the speeches in a scene without unplanned pauses between them.

piece - a scene, play, or literary work used for the basis of same.

places - a direction given to actors to prepare to enter or begin a scene.

playmaking - the creation of a dramatic scene or series of scenes.

plot - a diagram of placement and use of lights, costumes, sound, or other technical element.

plot elements - the incidents and ideas which tell the story.

polishing - rehearsing a scene to emphasize details such as exits, entrances, and the timing of specific lines and movements.

producer - person responsible for seeing that the production takes place.

production - the combined elements of artistic and technical creation necessary for a theater performance.

projection - "throwing" the voice the required distance in order to be heard.

prompt - to give an actor a line during rehearsal or performance.

prompt script - the script from which a performance is run. Includes all blocking notation, cue sheets, etc.

props - stage properties, that is, objects handled by actors during the course of a play.

proscenium - the opening of a conventional stage which separates actors and audience.

proscenium staging - a kind of staging in which all of the audience is seated directly opposite the playing area.

punchline - the last few words of a comedic speech.

R

race-thru - a rehearsal run at a greatly accelerated pace.

read-thru - reading a script aloud from beginning to end.

rehearsal - a practice performance of a play.

role - the character (or part) assigned to an actor.

run-thru - a rehearsal in which a play (or scene) is performed from beginning to end.

S

scenario - an outline or synopsis of a play.

script - a copy of the written text of a play.

set decoration - those non-functional finishing touches to any stage design which give it special character or mood, e.g pictures on the wall, knick knacks, books, plants, leaves on the ground.

stage directions - indications in the script of a play designating specific actions for the characters and technical directions.

stage manager - the person responsible for the smooth running of all aspects of a performance.

stage picture - the visual composition of set pieces, space, and actors at any given moment during a production.

subtext - implied but not spoken dialogue.

T

technical (or tech) rehearsal - a rehearsal, usually without actors, to rehearse set changes, light and sound cues.

techies - a slang term (not always complimentary) for members of the technical crew of a show.

telescope - leaving out details in a piece of action.

theatre games - acting exercises presented in a game format.

theatrical - (adj.) containing some or all of the elements of theatre; usually a heightened sense of light, color, sound, etc.

throw away - to give a line less than ordinary emphasis.

type casting - choosing an actor to play a role because he or she "looks the part."

U

upstage - at the rear of the stage, away from the audience.

upstage - (verb) an action taken by an actor which forces the actor playing opposite him or her to face upstage, away from the audience.

W

warm-up - any activity which prepares actors to act.

work-thru - a rehearsal in which stage and character business is worked on in detail.

working drawings - technical drawings of a stage property or piece of scenery indicating how it is to be constructed.

✓   *TIP:*   As you try various activities in this book and find that they work so well for you that you plan to use them again, jot down their names and page numbers on this sheet for handy reference.

A FINAL NOTE
ABOUT THE
ILLUSTRATIONS USED IN PLAYMAKING

Most of the illustrations in this book are from various volumes of clip art. The chapter heading illustrations are collages of clip art. Both teachers and students can create symbolic visual representations of concepts and ideas by using readily available clip art images in a collage, exercising their imaginations while enriching their aesthetic literacy.

Creative Educational Systems
P.O. Box 6659, East Brunswick, NJ 08816
Tel: 732-698-9885; Fax: 732-698-9886
EIN # 33-0422302 . Vendor . # cre018 . BOE# 7000149

Purchase Order #:   Invoice #:

           Invoice Date:

Bill to:	
Name:	
Address:	
City, State, Zip:	
Phone:	
Fax:	

	The New Playmaking books @	23.00 ea	
	Greek curriculum guides @	14.00 ea	
	Columbus curriculum guides @	12.00 ea	
	Mexican curriculum guides @	15.00 ea	
	Folklore Festival Special Edition guides @	12.00 ea	
	Folklore Festival plays @	7.00 ea	
	The Odyssey plays @	7.00 ea	
	Fairytale Festival plays @	7.00 ea	
	Jungle Book plays @	7.00 ea	
	Snow Queen plays @	7.00 ea	
	Dream Rehearsed plays @	7.00 ea	
	Coyote Tales plays @	7.00 ea	
	Eight Plays for a New Century @	30.00 ea	
	Two Fathom Mark Twain plays @	7.00 ea	
	Pre-tax Subtotal		
	Tax	Waived	
	Shipping and Handling	Included	
	TOTAL DUE:		
NOTE	10% Discount for orders of 20-50 of any one publication, 20% Discount for 50 and above		

Terms: Net 30
Please make checks payable to "Creative Educational Systems" at the above address.

Ordered on: Ordered by:
Institution:
Date Shipped:
Received:

EMPOWER THE CHILD TO LEARN!

"PLAYMAKING carries the banner in the march against apathy and fading self-esteem among today's youth. Its creative, purposeful, and easy-to-follow approach should stimulate teachers in every classroom in America and, in the process, establish CES as a pioneer of progressive education."

Richard K. Baron
Executive Director
Herman Goldman Foundation
NYC

"...a fine job of combining theory with practical application throughout the book... The chapter regarding the design of an arts-based thematic curriculum is an excellent source of information for today's classroom teacher... will act as a guideline for years to come. The attention to all the details of a production from stage managing to sound and music design should make any teacher's productions a manageable joy."

Paul Larson
Fine Arts Mentor, K-6,
Chino USD, CA

The New PLAYMAKING:
The Latest in Integrating the Arts into Education

"...A broad vision as well as the nitty-gritty to achieve it."

Marvin Axelrod
Teacher/Coordinator
of student activities
South Bronx HS, NYC

"The book is 'user-friendly' –it conjures up travel to have fun and explore, rather than a lockstep how-to-do approach."

Ivy Berchuck
Coordinator Gifted Program/
Cultural Arts
Forest Hills, NY

DISCOVER HOW TO:

Motivate your students to embrace learning.
Understand and apply the elements of creativity.
Design your own creative classroom.
Integrate every subject area with an arts-based thematic curriculum.
Dramatize children's literature, historical events, biographical materials, scientific concepts, even math principles!
Create a theatrical production with your students from the development of a script through the rehearsal process to the performance... and after!

"A highly imaginative work, inspiring to read... provides a wide range of practical 'how-to' methods, teaching strategies which will aid both the beginning and the experienced teacher to use the arts effectively as a dynamic teaching tool with joyful results."

Dr. Amanda Sue Rudisill
Professor of Theatre Arts
California State University
San Bernardino, CA

"PLAYMAKING is really about recreating our society at this critical moment in history."

Helen Marie Guditis
Executive Director
The Broadway Theatre Institute, NYC

ABOUT THE AUTHORS

The directors of Creative Educational Systems have been arts-in-education consultants for over fifteen years and have designed successful programs for thousands of teachers across the country. This book tells how they did it!

ISBN 0-942345-10-X
52000

9 780942 345100